DRAGON
Naturally Speaking®
for the Office Professional

Karl Barksdale
Technology Consultant
Provo, Utah

Michael Rutter
Christa McAuliffe Fellow
Brigham Young University

SOUTH-WESTERN
THOMSON LEARNING

Australia • Canada • Mexico • Singapore • Spain • United Kingdom • United States

SOUTH-WESTERN
™
THOMSON LEARNING

Dragon NaturallySpeaking® for the Office Professional
by Karl Barksdale and Michael Rutter

Executive Editor:
Karen Schmohe

Editor:
Martha Conway

Copy Editor:
Anne Noschang

Channel Coordinators:
Nancy Long, Chris McNamee

Marketing Coordinator:
Sharon Turner

Consulting Editor:
John Wills

Production Manager:
Jane Congdon

Manufacturing Manager:
Carol Chase

Art and Design Coordinator:
Michelle Kunkler

Permissions Editor:
Linda Ellis

Cover Design:
Grannan Graphic Design

Internal Design:
Grannan Graphic Design

Compositor:
electro-publishing

Printer:
Courier, Kendalville, Inc.

For more information, contact
South-Western Educational Publishing
5101 Madison Road
Cincinnati, OH 45227-1490.
Or you can visit our internet site at
www.swep.com.

For permission to use material from this text or product, contact us by
Phone: 1-800-730-2214
Fax: 1-800-730-2215
www.thomsonrights.com

Your Course Planning Just Got Easier!

Century 21 Keyboarding & Information Processing
by Robinson, Hoggatt, Shank, Beaumont, Crawford, and Erickson

Put 75 years of keyboarding experience to work for you! Learn the keyboarding and computer application skills necessary for success in today's technology-driven world.

0-538-69155-7	Complete Course
0-538-69156-5	Book One, Lessons 1-150

Corporate View
by Barksdale and Rutter

Students, working as interns, rotate through the major departments of a large corporation, using the live corporate Intranet site, www.corpview.com, to gather information and develop skills. Look for new titles in this series of applications textbook/simulations that build on the Orientation book!

0-538-68471-2	Orientation Text
0-538-72285-1	Orientation Text & CD
0-538-69153-0	Corporate Communications Text
0-538-69290-1	Corporate Communications Text & CD
0-538-69154-9	Marketing, Sales, and Support Text
0-538-69291-X	Marketing, Sales, and Support Text & CD

College Keyboarding
by VanHuss, Duncan, Forde, and Woo

Use this winning combination of skill building and Windows word processing instruction to develop keyboarding and computer skills.

0-538-72248-7	Keyboarding Course, Lessons 1-30
0-538-72250-9	Keyboarding and Formatting, Lessons 1-60 — Microsoft Word 2000
0-538-72249-5	Complete Course, Lessons 1-180 — Microsoft Office 2000
0-538-72254-1	Keyboarding and Formatting, Lessons 1-60 — WordPerfect 9
0-538-72253-3	Complete Course, Lessons 1-180 — WordPerfect Office 2000

Join Us on the Internet
www.swep.com

SOUTH-WESTERN
THOMSON LEARNING

NEW! *L&H Voice Xpress™ for the Office Professional*
by Barksdale and Rutter

Speech software is revolutionizing legal, medical, dental, government, and business offices everywhere! You can be part of the excitement with *L&H Voice Xpress™ for the Office Professional*.

0-538-72370-X Text
0-538-72373-4 Instructor's Manual

NEW! *IBM® ViaVoice™ for the Office Professional*
by Barksdale and Rutter

Voice typing is transforming the way people work, write, and enter data. *IBM® ViaVoice™ for the Office Professional* will teach you how to use this new software and apply it to various office applications.

0-538-72372-6 Text
0-538-72373-4 Instructor's Manual

NEW! *Dragon NaturallySpeaking® for the Office Professional*
by Barksdale and Rutter

Learn the most effective way to use the *Dragon NaturallySpeaking®* software — by using real-world applications in the classroom. This book takes you step-by-step through the speech learning process.

0-538-72371-8 Text
0-538-72373-4 Instructor's Manual

Join Us on the Internet
www.swep.com

Using This Book

Sections

This text is divided into five sections. The first two sections focus on basic speech recognition skills. Subsequent sections apply speaking solutions in business, medical, and legal office communications.

Lessons

The first two sections contain Lessons that focus on learning the essentials of a specific speech recognition software program.

Step-by-Step Instructions

Instructions take you step-by-step through speech learning process.

Activities

The last three sections contain Activities that will have you applying your voice skills to true-to-life working situations derived from marketing, medical, legal, and corporate communications careers.

Speaking About...

The *Speaking About ...* segments throughout the text are activities designed to improve your writing and business communications skills.

FYI

For Your Information tips provide hints and advice that enhance the step-by-step instructions.

Speaking Solutions Reference Card

A command reference card is provided that will help you remember everything you have learned about using your software. The card is referenced throughout the text. Look for the references next to the double checks.

www.speakingabout.com

To help you get the most out of your course, additional speech recognition lessons, answers to the Speaking About quizzes, and definitions for all those technical terms you will need to tackle as a speech recognition user are provided at our online site.

Speech will increase your productivity, help you avoid injury, and improve your writing and communications skills. Enter www.speakingabout.com into your Internet Explorer or Netscape browser, click the link for your speech recognition software, and take advantage of these additional online resources.

Preface

Speech recognition is reshaping writing, data input, and record keeping in medical, dental, legal, and other offices around the world. There are three great reasons for you to learn your speech recognition software, starting today! Speech software can:

- Increase your productivity
- Help you avoid injury or overcome a handicap
- Improve your writing

Increase Your Productivity

Voice-typing is transforming the way people work, write, and enter data in professional offices around the globe. With speech recognition software: doctors and medical staffs can complete medical reports and patient charts in less time; lawyers and paralegals can finish legal briefs faster; corporate executives can voice-type their corporate communications, saving their administrative assistants hours of extra keyboarding; journalists can meet their deadlines more easily by voice-writing; and students can finish their term papers more quickly.

In the field of medical transcription, speech recognition has been increasing productivity by:

- Lowering costs by eliminating transcription charges
- Increasing accuracy
- Saving report preparation time
- Making it easier to comply with insurance requirements and government regulations
- Reducing absenteeism among medical transcriptionists and medical office employees due to Carpal Tunnel Syndrome (CTS) and Repetitive Stress Injuries (RSI).

Help You Avoid Injury or Overcome a Handicap

Speech recognition software has helped those with physical limitations overcome their disabilities. For example, in 1997, a student with cerebral palsy was limited in his ability to type. He quickly overcame this limitation by learning his voice recognition software and became the fastest typist in his school. Moreover, during the past three years, speech recognition has moved beyond a specialized tool for those unable to type to a mainstream solution to reduce computer-related injuries.

Keyboards should come with warning labels from the Surgeon General reading, *"Repetitive use of the keyboard and mouse can be painful and potentially hazardous to your hands, arms, shoulders, neck, and back."*

Carpal Tunnel Syndrome (CTS) and Repetitive Stress Injuries (RSI) have reached epidemic proportions due to ergonomically incorrect equipment (including work stations, chairs, monitor location, and keyboards); a dramatic increase in the amount of typing and clicking people do; and a two-decade-long trend that has encouraged children to use the keyboard and mouse at increasingly young ages.

For many, the pain caused by RSI or CTS has become an expected part of their working lives. The bottom line is this: The more *you* type and click, the more susceptible *you* will be to these types of injuries. At some point, if you type and click frequently enough, you may begin feeling pain yourself. And you will instinctively ask yourself the question, "Is this pain necessary?"

No! Pain isn't a fact of life in the information age. There is an alternative. The RSI and CTS epidemic can end quickly if computer users learn to use speech recognition tools effectively.

The most effective prevention requires reducing the number of repetitive keystrokes and mouse clicks you do. Speech software can easily reduce the amount of keyboarding by 50 percent for nearly every computer user—including you. This alone will significantly reduce RSI and CTS problems related to the use of the keyboard and mouse. Those who already suffer pain can reduce their typing and clicking by 95 percent or more if they choose to do so.

Improve Your Writing

The third benefit of speech recognition software may be the most important. For many people, slow keyboarding gets in the way of their ability to express themselves in writing. Slow keyboarding interrupts the flow of ideas, and writing may suffer as a result. In the *Speaking About…*sections of this text, we explore ways to help you write better by channeling your thoughts quickly through your voice software to the printed word.

 For more information about RSI, CTS, and your speech software, visit www.speakingabout.com.

Table of Contents

Section 1 | BASIC NaturallySpeaking SOLUTIONS

Section 2 | SPEECH-WRITING AND FORMATTING SOLUTIONS

Section 3 | SPEAKING SOLUTIONS FOR YOUR CAREER

Section 4 | SPEAKING SOLUTIONS IN THE MEDICAL MARKET

section 1

Basic NaturallySpeaking Solutions

Lesson 1 | UP AND RUNNING
Lesson 2 | PRACTICING YOUR ENUNCIATION
   Speaking About . . .   EVALUATING YOUR SPEED AND ACCURACY
Lesson 3 | CORRECTING SPEECH ERRORS IMMEDIATELY
Lesson 4 | TRAINING SPEECH ERRORS PERMANENTLY
   Speaking About . . .   PROOFREADING AND EDITING

Writing at the speed of your thoughts is an amazing experience—challenging, but amazing. With Dragon NaturallySpeaking® by Lernout & Hauspie™, your writing isn't limited by your keying speed or the pace of your pencil across a notepad. You can think, speak, and write at the same time. Speech recognition is a powerful new tool for business, personal productivity, and writing. It's time for you to learn how to use it. And it won't take you very long to master the basic skills.

In this book, you will apply your speech recognition skills to true-to-life writing tasks like those performed every day by professionals in medical, legal, and business offices. You'll input data into a computer at the speed of speech. You'll become more efficient, more employable, and you'll probably enjoy writing much, much more.

Your biggest challenge won't be in learning to use your software, but in remembering all of those writing tips your English and business teachers kept lecturing you about. In the *Speaking About* sections we will remind you of what they told you.

So relax, get comfortable, adjust your microphone, and let's start.

Lesson 1 | *Up and Running*

OBJECTIVES In this lesson you will …

(A) Adjust Your Microphone Position
(B) Complete Your Enrollment Training
(C) Choose Your User Profile
(D) Readjust Your Audio Settings
(E) Protect Your Voice

Consistency is the key to accurate speech recognition. Always do the following:

- Adjust your microphone position
- Complete your enrollment
- Choose your user profile
- Readjust your audio settings
- Protect your voice

The enrollment process "trains" your computer to understand your voice. Training greatly increases your accuracy and makes voice-typing easier to do. The next few pages will walk you through this essential activity.

A Adjust Your Microphone Position

Start by placing your microphone in the proper position. With a headset, follow the "rule of thumb": Place the microphone a thumb's width away from the side of your mouth (see Figure 1-1). If your specific headset microphone's boom or arm is too long to stay at the side of your mouth, place the microphone even with or slightly below your lower lip so the microphone does not pick up your breathing.

Make sure the listening portion of your microphone is facing toward your mouth. This is often marked with a dot or some other marking, such as the word *Voice*. **NOTE:** With a freestanding microphone, you should be within two feet of the receiving device.

Don't touch the microphone end with your hands or with your mouth. It is also best if you can obtain your own personal headset that you can use every day.

Place your microphone in the same position every time you use your speech software. If you notice "breathing errors" (if extra words appear because of your breathing), move your microphone more to the side of your mouth or slightly further down below your lower lip.

figure 1-1

Position Your Microphone

1a

☑ Double-check Section 1a on your Dragon NaturallySpeaking reference card at the end of this book if you need to review microphone adjustment hints.

B Complete Your Enrollment Training

To get the most out of your speech system, you must create and use your own personal speech profile. This is accomplished through the enrollment or "training" process. Training will create your personal speaker profile, which will be different from every other personal profile on the planet. This is *your* voice database, recording the way you speak and memorizing the unique words you use.

Enrollment will:

- Set your initial microphone settings
- Analyze your unique way of speaking

1. Start Dragon NaturallySpeaking by selecting **Start→Programs→Dragon NaturallySpeaking.**

2. The enrollment steps differ depending on whether you are the first or later user of the software:

First User: If you are the first user of NaturallySpeaking on your computer, your software will walk you step by step through the enrollment training process. Jump to Step 3 for a few helpful hints.

Second User: If you are the second user on the system, choose the **NaturallySpeaking** menu from the DragonBar; then choose **Advanced→Manage Users,** as shown in Figure 1-2. (You may instead select **Users→Manage Users**, as shown in Figure 1-3.) Continue to Step 3.

Third or Later User: If you are the third or later user of NaturallySpeaking, select **New** from the **Manage Users** dialog box, as shown in Figure 1-4 below.

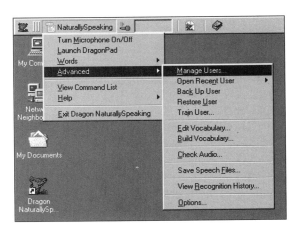

figure 1-2

Open the **Manage Users** Dialog Box from the **NaturallySpeaking** Menu on the DragonBar

New button

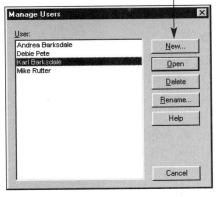

figure 1-3

You Can Also Open the **Manage Users** Dialog Box from the **Users** Menu on the DragonBar.

figure 1-4

Choose **New** from the **Manage Users** Dialog Box

3. Review the steps you will follow. During training you will:

- Create your user speech profile
- Adjust your microphone
- Train NaturallySpeaking to understand your way of speaking
- View the tutorial
- Start using NaturallySpeaking

4. Begin training your software by entering your name into the system (see Figure 1-5).

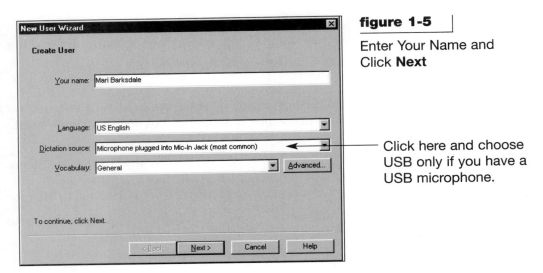

figure 1-5

Enter Your Name and
Click **Next**

Click here and choose
USB only if you have a
USB microphone.

F Y I   If you're using a USB microphone, you will need to change the dictation source before you continue. Do this by clicking the down arrow and choosing the **USB** option in the **Dictation source** line, as displayed in Figure 1-5.

---

5. Click **Next** to continue.

6. You will need to read the on-screen instructions and click **Next** to move from step to step. There are three essential phases in this process: adjusting your volume level, adjusting your microphone settings, and analyzing your speech. Let's review them one at a time as you move through the steps.

   a. Adjust your initial volume level: NaturallySpeaking will automatically run its Audio Setup Wizard and fine-tune its microphone settings. The first stage adjusts the volume level. As you read a selection of text, this check is performed automatically. Watch the volume slider move down as the system adjusts to your voice (see Figure 1-6).

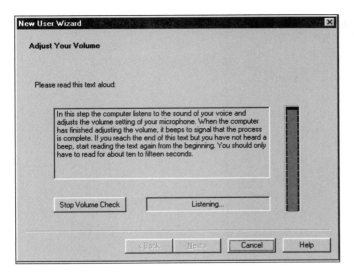

figure 1-6

NaturallySpeaking Will Adjust the Volume Level of Your Microphone

b. **Adjust your initial microphone settings:** NaturallySpeaking will now calculate the quality of your sound system. This check determines whether your computer's hardware and microphone are adequate for speech recognition. This is an essential measure of your system's ability to perform. Click the **Start Quality Check** button and read the paragraph as instructed (see Figure 1-7). The quality check is performed automatically as you read. (Click the **Stop Quality Check** button if you need to cough or sneeze, or wish to start over, then continue reading again when you are ready.) NaturallySpeaking will tell you how your audio system is performing. Your system should record a level of *Adequate* or higher.

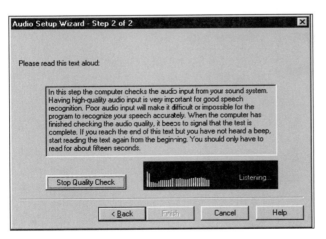

figure 1-7

NaturallySpeaking Will Run a Quality Check of Your Audio System

c. **Analyze your unique way of speaking:** Once the audio levels have been set for your voice, the system is ready to analyze your speech. To do this, follow the online instructions. You will start by reading several screens aloud. Start reading at the arrow, as shown in Figure 1-8.

figure 1-8

Read the Screens by
Following the Arrow

F Y I When training, speak with your normal, clear voice, the way you intend to talk to your computer in the future. Try to say each word clearly while reading each sentence without pausing.

7. When you come to the **Select Text** window (Figure 1-9), select a story, click **OK**, and start reading in your normal dictation voice. Follow the arrow as you read aloud (see Figure 1-10). If you need to pause to rest or get a drink, click the **Pause** button. However, you should try to finish all of the reading in one sitting.

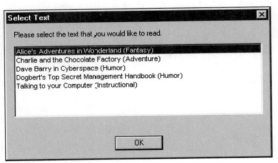

figure 1-9

Select a Story and Begin
Reading

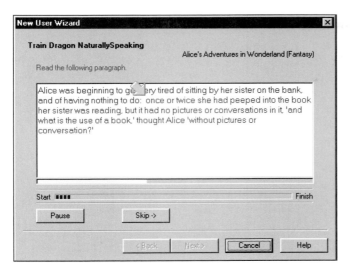

figure 1-10

NaturallySpeaking Keeps
Track of Your Progress as
You Read

8. If NaturallySpeaking gets lost, falls behind, or gets confused, it will point to the next word it wants you to say, as shown in Figure 1-10. Start reading again from the arrow. If you can't seem to say a word correctly, skip it by clicking the **Skip** button.

9. When you have finished reading, click **OK**.

You may read additional stories, or you can have Dragon NaturallySpeaking analyze your speech now (see Figure 1-11). For most beginners with clear speech, one reading is usually sufficient. However, if you have a distinct accent or want to achieve the highest level of accuracy possible, you can read additional text into the system at any time by clicking **NaturallySpeaking→Advanced→Train User**.

figure 1-11

Click **OK** and the System
Will Analyze Your Unique
Way of Speaking

10. Take a few minutes and start the tutorial (see Figure 1-12). It's interesting, and it will help you understand more about using NaturallySpeaking.

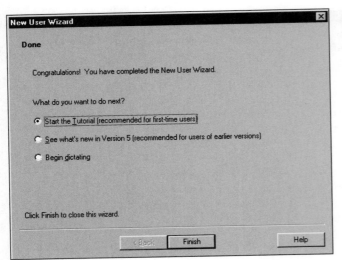

figure 1-12

Run the Tutorial

1b

☑ **Double-check** Section 1b on your NaturallySpeaking reference card at the end of this book if you forget the enrollment steps.

Ⓒ Choose Your User Profile

You must ALWAYS use your own personal voice profile! Don't accidentally use the profile of another person, or your accuracy will plummet and you may inadvertently add inaccurate words to another person's voice model.

1c

☑ **Double-check** your NaturallySpeaking reference card if you forget how to switch to your personal voice profile.

Ⓓ Readjust Your Audio Settings

Your voice profile automatically remembers your audio settings from session to session. However, you should readjust your audio settings if one of the following occurs:

- Your background noise or acoustic conditions change
- There is a noticeable decline in your recognition accuracy
- Another person has used the speech recognition system before you

To run the Audio Setup Wizard:

1. Open NaturallySpeaking and click or say *(Click) NaturallySpeaking→Advanced→Check Audio*.

2. Read and follow the instructions. Press the **Next** button to continue from screen to screen.

The command **Click** is optional when you are saying menu items or clicking buttons. If a spoken word or command is shown in parentheses in this book, it is optional. Say **Click** if NaturallySpeaking doesn't seem to understand your command without it. For example, start by saying **NaturallySpeaking**. If the menu doesn't open immediately, say **Click NaturallySpeaking**.

1d

☑ **Double-check** your NaturallySpeaking reference card if you forget the Check Audio steps.

E Protect Your Voice

One of the benefits of using speech recognition software is that it reduces your risk of developing serious Carpal Tunnel Syndrome (CTS) in your hands and Repetitive Stress Injuries (RSI) to your hands, wrists, arms, or shoulders. However, voice-typing can place an added strain on your vocal cords! Keep your water bottle handy and take constant sips. Take frequent breaks from talking. (Don't let repetitive vocal cord injuries replace repetitive stress injuries!)

F Y I   For more information on CTS and RSI, visit **www.speakingabout.com**.

Lesson 2 | *Practicing Your Enunciation*

OBJECTIVES   In this lesson you will . . .

(A) Speak Microphone Commands Clearly

(B) Speak Words Clearly

(C) Clear the Screen

(D) Speak Line and Paragraph Commands Clearly

(E) Speak Punctuation Clearly and Listen to Your Speech

(F) Save Documents

Speaking About . . . Evaluating Speed and Accuracy

(G) Transfer Your NaturallySpeaking Skills to Microsoft Word or Corel WordPerfect

Practice speaking clearly, smoothly, and deliberately. You will need to practice enunciating words, commands, and punctuation. When you speak, follow these rules:

- Say each word, command, and punctuation mark clearly.

- Speak in a normal tone of voice. Your software works best when you speak naturally.

- Don't worry if your words fail to appear immediately as you say them. Your software will catch up to you soon enough.

A Speak Microphone Commands Clearly

Follow these rules when saying commands:

- Pause slightly before and after commands.

  Say <pause> **Go to Sleep** *<pause>*

- When there are several words in a command, say the command more as a phrase than as separate words. Don't stop in the middle of a multiword command.

  Say **Go to Sleep**, *not* **Go** *<pause>* **to** *<pause>* **sleep**

- Clearly say each word in the command. Don't rush or slur commands.

  Say **Go to Sleep**, *not* **Gotosleep**

- Don't shout and don't whisper commands. Use a normal tone of voice.

  Say **Go to Sleep**, *not* **GO TO SLEEP!** *or go to sleep*

1. Open NaturallySpeaking by selecting **Start→Programs→Dragon NaturallySpeaking**.

2. If there are multiple users on your computer system, select your name from the **Manage Users** dialog box (see Figure 1-13), and click **Open**. If you are the only user of NaturallySpeaking on your computer, skip to Step 3.

figure 1-13

Select Your Name from the
Manage Users Dialog Box

3. Click the **Microphone** button on the DragonBar with your mouse to turn NaturallySpeaking's microphone on, as shown in Figure 1-14.

figure 1-14

The NaturallySpeaking
DragonBar and the
Microphone Button

4. This first command will pause the microphone. Say this:

Go to Sleep

 If you have any difficulty making any of these voice commands work properly, press the control key (**Ctrl**) as you say the command. This will force NaturallySpeaking to recognize what you say as a command and not as text.

5. This next command will wake the microphone up again. Try this:

Wake Up

6. This next command will turn the microphone completely off. Try this:

Microphone Off

7. Click the microphone back on again by pressing the **+** key on your numeric keypad.

8. Turn your microphone off again by pressing the **+** key on your numeric keypad again.

You can display the DragonBar in several different ways by first clicking on the **Dragon** icon in the top left-hand corner of the DragonBar, then choosing a mode from the drop-down menu. For beginners, the **Docked to Top Mode** is recommended, as shown in Figure 1-15. If you accidentally get stuck in the **Tray Icon Only Mode**, right-click on the microphone found in the tray on the Windows Start Bar and return the system to the **Docked to Top Mode**.

figure 1-15

Click the Dragon Icon to Change How the DragonBar Is Displayed

Double-check your NaturallySpeaking reference card if you forget the microphone commands.

B Speak Words Clearly

Don't worry about correcting mistakes when practicing your enunciation. You will learn to correct mistakes in Lessons 3 and 4. Until then, just practice speaking clearly and continuously. Everyone makes mistakes in the beginning. Simply enunciate each sentence again, concentrating on the way you say words and phrases. Remember these rules:

- Speak each word clearly.
- Don't break words into syllables. For instance, say **popcorn**, not **pop corn**.
- Don't run words together. Say **candy bar**, not **canybr**.
- Continue talking until you reach the end of your sentence, thought, or idea. Speak each word strongly.
- Don't speak too fast. Don't speak too slowly. Speak at a speed that is just right for you!
- If a lot of extra words randomly appear, like *the, we, but*, and the word *and*, chances are your microphone is too close to your nose or mouth and it is picking up your breathing. Move the microphone slightly down or more to the side of your mouth and redo your audio check again by saying *(Click) NaturallySpeaking→Advanced→Check Audio*.
- Don't shout and don't whisper. Don't let your speaking volume trail off toward the end of a sentence.

1. Wake up NaturallySpeaking, open the DragonPad word processing program, and put NaturallySpeaking to sleep again with the following commands:

Say *Wake Up* (or press the **+** key on your numeric keypad)

Say *Start DragonPad*

Say *Go to Sleep* (or press the **+** key on your numeric keypad)

You may also open DragonPad by clicking the **Start DragonPad** icon on the DragonBar (see Figure 1-16) or by selecting the **NaturallySpeaking** menu and choosing **Launch DragonPad**.

2. Review the features of DragonPad and some of the other elements you will see as you use NaturallySpeaking. (See Figure 1-16.)

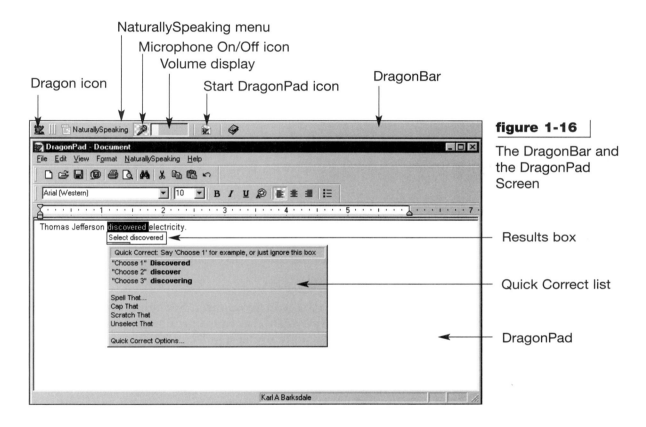

NaturallySpeaking menu
Microphone On/Off icon
Volume display
Start DragonPad icon
DragonBar
Dragon icon

figure 1-16

The DragonBar and the DragonPad Screen

Results box

Quick Correct list

DragonPad

3. Say the following sentences in DragonPad. Say each *Period* as you come to it. It often helps to pause slightly before and after you say each *Period*.

Say *Wake Up* (or press the **+** key on your numeric keypad)

Talk to your computer *Period* Speak normally and say each word clearly *Period* Don't shout and don't whisper *Period* Don't stop in the middle of a sentence *Period* Practice speaking clearly *Period*

Say *Go to Sleep* (or press the **+** key on your numeric keypad)

4. Some speakers run words together, which causes unnecessary errors. For example, many say **inthemiddleof** instead of saying **in the middle of**. Wake up your microphone and try the paragraph *one more time*, concentrating on the sounds or pronunciation of the words you missed the first time. See if you can improve your accuracy, and then move on to Part C.

When you wish to rest or to talk to someone, use the *Go to Sleep* or *Microphone Off* command to pause the microphone. Otherwise, your system will keep listening for words, and you may be surprised at the mess that can appear on your screen!

2b

☑ **Double-check** your NaturallySpeaking reference card if you forget how to speak words clearly.

ⓒ Clear the Screen

Clearing the screen by deleting the existing text or by opening a new document is important for many of the future activities. Clearing the screen is a simple task.

To clear the screen:

- *Say **Select All** or **Select Document***
- *Say **Delete That***

To open a new document:

- *Say **(Click) File, New** or click **File→New** with your mouse.*

1. Try to say the following text. Remember to say each *Period* as you come to it:

Say *Wake Up* (or press the **+** key on your numeric keypad)

Don't break any speed records when you speak to your computer. Speaking fast will cause you to run words together. Speaking slowly can also cause problems. If you speak very fast or very slowly, the system will have trouble understanding you. Talk at a speed that is just right for you.

2. Click your insertion point (the flashing vertical line) at the end of the paragraph. Now say:

Select All or *Select Document*

Delete That

Say *Go to Sleep* (or press the **+** key on your numeric keypad)

You may have noticed a little box with words constantly changing as you speak. This is called the Results Box. The Results Box lets you see what your computer is thinking as it processes your speech. If you find the Results Box distracting, you can click and drag it to a more appropriate spot on your screen. You can also anchor it there by right-clicking the **Results Box** and selecting the **Anchor** option. From that point on, the Results Box will remain in the exact portion of the screen that you have selected.

2c

☑ **Double-check** your NaturallySpeaking reference card if you forget how to clear the screen.

D Speak Line and Paragraph Commands Clearly

The *New Paragraph* and *New Line* commands are essential. *New Paragraph* is equivalent to pressing the Enter key twice to create a double space. *New Line* moves the insertion point (the flashing line) down to the next line in the document. This is like pressing the Enter key one time to create a single space.

1. Clear your screen (refer back to Part C if necessary). Wake up your microphone and practice these new commands by saying each sentence. Remember not to stop in the middle of a sentence! Try this:

Say *Wake Up* (or press the **+** key on your numeric keypad)

This is a complete sentence *Period New Line*
Speak clearly without stopping *Period New Line*
Speak in a normal voice *Period New Paragraph*

Say *Go to Sleep* (or press the **+** key on your numeric keypad)

F Y I Sometimes we cut off the final sounds of words, such as saying *New Paragra* instead of *New ParagraPH*. Be sure to say the entire word or command clearly. Also, if you have trouble with a spoken command, simply hold the **Ctrl** key down as you say it. This will force NaturallySpeaking to only recognize what you say as a command. Alternatively, if you want to display text instead of a command, hold the **Shift** key down. This will force NaturallySpeaking to display the words you say as text, even if what you are saying is a command.

---

2. Clear your screen again and try the following sentences. Speak clearly, and say each word and *Period*. Don't rush! Say **an appropriate,** not **anappropriate**. Don't speak too slowly, which may cause you to break words into syllables. Say **documents**, not **doc u ments**.

Wake Up

Think about your audience. *New Line*
Evaluate your purpose in writing. *New Line*
Use an appropriate writing style or personality. *New Line*
Don't make your documents very long. *New Paragraph*

Go to Sleep

3. Clear your screen again and practice the *New Paragraph* command with some familiar phrases. Practice saying each word clearly. Most people tend to run the words together, as in **Timeflies whenyur havn fun**. Try saying each word distinctly!

Wake Up

Time flies when you are having fun.

Don't rock the boat.

The early bird catches the worm.

Speak clearly without stopping in the middle of your sentences.

Try to say each word clearly.

Go to Sleep

2d

✓Double-check your NaturallySpeaking reference card if you forget the line and paragraph commands.

E Speak Punctuation Clearly and Listen to Your Speech

With today's speech software you must say punctuation marks. Let's practice the following punctuation marks:

- *Period* creates a (.)
- *Comma* creates a (,)
- *Question Mark* creates a (?)
- *Exclamation Point/Mark* creates a (!)
- *Colon* creates a (:)
- *Semicolon* creates a (;)
- *Dash* creates a (-)
- *Open Quote* creates a beginning quote (")
- *Close Quote* creates an ending quote (")

Now practice these commands for listening to and moving through a document:

- To listen to your document, say **Read Document**, or select the text and say **Read That** (**NOTE:** These two commands only work with the *Preferred* and *Professional* versions of Dragon NaturallySpeaking.)
- *Go to Top*
- *Go to Bottom*
- *Go/Move to Beginning of Line*
- *Go/Move to End of Line*

1. Clear your screen and practice punctuation marks by saying the next few sentences. Try each sentence two times, working to improve your enunciation of the words:

Wake Up

Is that your final answer?

Congratulations! You have just won the grand prize.

Do you want to buy a new computer?

I know what you want: a dog, a cat, and a tropical fish.

Don't speak very fast; don't speak very slowly; speak at just the right speed for you.

I think this is going rather well – better than expected!

"By the way, Michael, using NaturallySpeaking is easy."

Go to Sleep

2. Clear your screen again and try the following punctuated paragraphs. **NOTE:** Say each paragraph in this one-sided conversation before taking a break and reviewing the result. Don't stop in the middle of any sentence.

Wake Up

"May I help you? We have some wonderful items on sale today. Our prices are the best – the very best!

"We have popcorn, peanuts, and candy bars of all kinds. We also sell oranges, apples, apricots, bananas, plums, and peaches. Do you want any of our fabulous foods?

Why not? What do you mean I'm a pushy salesperson? Leave this establishment immediately! If you don't like apples, you can't stay here.

"Goodbye!"

Go to Sleep

3. Clear your screen and try the paragraphs above *once more*. Try to improve the way you say the words you may have missed the first time. The last time you say them, LEAVE the sentences on the screen and move to the next step.

4. Try moving your insertion point around your document with the following commands. Watch where the insertion point goes after you say each command:

Go to Top
Go to Bottom
Go to Top

Go to End of Line
Go to Beginning of Line

5. Try moving your insertion point with the following alternative commands. Watch the insertion point. Click on the first sentence and say:

Move to End of Document
Move to Beginning of Document
Move to End of Line
Move to Beginning of Line

6. This next command only works with the *Preferred* and *Professional* versions of Dragon NaturallySpeaking. You can't use this feature on the current *Standard* or *Essential* version of the software. If you have the Preferred or Professional version, or a version that is compatible with this feature, you can listen to the above document by saying:

Read Document

or

Select All
Read That

2e

Double-check your NaturallySpeaking reference card if you need to review how to say punctuation marks, listen to your document, or move around in a document.

F Save Documents

Saving files is obviously essential. With some versions of NaturallySpeaking you can save files using voice commands, but with other versions you can't. In the latter case, you must use your mouse.

- *Say (Click) File <pause> Save or Save As. Name the file and say (Click) Save.*
- *Alternative: Choose File→Save or Save As. Name the file and choose Save.*

1. Clear your screen and try the following sentences. Sometimes abbreviations for state names will appear, like *Fla.* for *Florida*. Here is another voice writing tip. Don't break long words into syllables. For example, say **Tallahassee**, not **Tal la has see**.

New York, New York.
I want to visit New York in the fall.

Paris, France.
I love Paris in the spring!

Tallahassee, Florida.
My parents live in Tallahassee in the winter.

Portland, Oregon.
Portland is pretty in the summer.

2. Save the document as **Seasons**.

Say *(Click) File* <pause> *Save*

Say *Seasons* to name the file

(**NOTE:** You may need to select a file format. A good choice is *Rich Text Format*, which can be read by both Microsoft Word and Corel WordPerfect.)

Say *(Click) Save*

Alternative saving method: Choose **File, Save** with your mouse. Name the file as **Seasons** and choose **Save.**

3. Clear your screen and try the following dialog.

I want to visit the following North American cities:

Seattle, Toronto, Chicago, Atlanta, Dallas, Boston, Denver, Baltimore, Mexico City, Miami.

4. Save the file as **Cities** using the steps listed on your reference card.

2f

✔**Double-check** your NaturallySpeaking reference card if you forget how to save.

Speaking About...

Evaluating Speed and Accuracy

In traditional keyboarding classes, teachers normally counted every five characters as a word. This formula makes evaluating keying ability consistent from one person to another. The formula counts spaces.

Chances are, based on this keyboarding formula, you are already speaking 110-140 words per minute or even faster! A quick way to measure your speed is to count the number of characters you can say in a minute. If you can speak 500 characters in a minute, you're entering text at 100 words per minute. In the two paragraphs in Step 1 there are approximately 250 characters. If you can say both paragraphs in 30 seconds or less, you are speaking faster than 100 words per minute. Not bad—not bad at all!

1. Start timing yourself as you say *Wake Up* or as you press the **+** key on your numeric keypad. Stop the clock when you say *Go to Sleep*. Try this:

Who will read your message? It is critical to know exactly who your audience is. Is it a friend or a business client? Your message must be directed to this audience.

Always have an exact reader in mind when you write. This is your target audience!

2. Did you break 100 words per minute? More importantly, how was your accuracy? Reread the two paragraphs in Step 1 again while concentrating on saying each word and sentence clearly without stopping in the middle of your sentences. Try to say all the words correctly, but don't speak too slowly. Use a comfortable speaking pace.

Ⓖ Transfer Your NaturallySpeaking Skills to Microsoft Word or Corel WordPerfect

Most experienced NaturallySpeaking users agree that it is best to learn the basic commands using DragonPad before jumping into a powerful word processor like Word or WordPerfect. And there are several reasons why:

- To use Microsoft Word or Corel WordPerfect effectively with your voice, you should consider the *Preferred* or higher edition of the software. The *Standard* version of NaturallySpeaking will allow you to dictate into these programs, but will not allow you the versatility you may need.

- Word or WordPerfect requires considerable extra memory and processor speed to run concurrently with NaturallySpeaking. Without a speedy computer or 128 MB of RAM, it might be best to stick with DragonPad and continue on to Lesson 3.

- Particularly with Word, there are many natural language technology (NLT) commands that can confuse a new user. It's best to learn the basic commands before moving into a powerful word processor like Microsoft Word.

- It takes experience to know whether a mistake is a word processing error or a speech error. Therefore, learning the basics with DragonPad first will help you understand these differences.

All these cautions having been said, if you have the *Standard*, *Preferred*, or a higher version of NaturallySpeaking and if Word or WordPerfect is installed properly on your computer, it's time to experiment. Use the following steps to transfer your speech skills to Word or WordPerfect. Look for this section at the end of future lessons in this book.

1. Close DragonPad and any other open applications on your desktop.

2. Turn on your NaturallySpeaking microphone by clicking the **Microphone On/Off** button.

3. Open Microsoft Word (or WordPerfect) by saying:

Start Microsoft Word   ***(Start WordPerfect)***

4. Repeat the timing found in the *Speaking About... Evaluating Speed and Accuracy* section. How does your accuracy in Word or WordPerfect compared to that in DragonPad?

5. Try some of the exercises you have previously completed in this lesson using Microsoft Word or WordPerfect instead of DragonPad:

- Try the microphone commands found in Part A (*Speak Microphone Commands Clearly*).

- Review the dialogue in Part B (*Speak Words Clearly*).

- Try clearing your screen with the commands found in Part C (*Clear the Screen*).

- Practice the ***Line*** and ***Paragraph*** commands found in Part D (*Speak Line and Paragraph Commands Clearly*).

- Attempt the punctuation commands and listen to your speech in Word or WordPerfect by reviewing Part E (*Speak Punctuation Clearly and Listen to Your Speech*).

- Practice saving a document in Microsoft Word or WordPerfect using the commands found in Part F (*Save Documents*).

6. Close your word processing program with the following voice commands:

(Click) File

Exit

Lesson 3 | *Correcting Speech Errors Immediately*

OBJECTIVES In this lesson you will . . .

(A) Scratch or Undo Errors Immediately

(B) Substitute Words

(C) Deselect Words and Use *Resume With*

(D) Select and Delete Errors

(E) Select Again

(F) Spell Web and Email Addresses and the Alphabet

(G) Transfer Your NaturallySpeaking Skills to Microsoft Word or Corel WordPerfect

Computers make mistakes, and lots of them! Most errors can be corrected quickly and painlessly using a variety of techniques.

A Scratch or Undo Errors Immediately

To quickly erase the last word or continuous phrase that you have spoken, use the *Scratch That* command. *Undo That* will undo the last mistake or correction you have just dictated.

1. Open NaturallySpeaking. (**NOTE:** Make sure to choose your user name from the **Manage Users** dialog box.) Click the microphone button, say the sentence below, and try the *Scratch That* command. You don't need to correct your mistakes because you are just going to erase the words anyway.

In the morning after a walk, he loved to eat bacon, eggs, and toast.

Scratch That
Scratch That
Scratch That
Continue saying *Scratch That* *until all the text has been eliminated.*

2. The *Scratch That* and *Undo That* commands both remove the last chunk of text that you have spoken continuously. However, *Undo That* works slightly differently from *Scratch That* because it can reinstate deleted text as well. Try another sentence, use both commands, and observe the difference.

"In the meantime, Todd, let's start working on that business plan. We must have it ready for the meeting on Thursday."

Scratch That
Undo That
Undo That
Undo That

> ✔ **Double-check** your NaturallySpeaking reference card if you forget the scratch and undo options.

B Substitute Words

At times you'll wish to substitute one word for another. The substitution technique is one of the most popular ways to correct words you may have misspoken. To substitute a word or words, say:

- *Select <word or words>*
- (Say the new word or words)

> **F Y I** Don't pause between the command *Select* and the word you are selecting. For example, say *Select* **Benjamin**, not *Select* <pause> **Benjamin**.

1. Clear your screen and try this:

Benjamin Franklin discovered electricity.

Select **Benjamin** <pause> **Thomas**

Select **Franklin** <pause> **Jefferson**

Select **discovered** <pause> **invented**

Select **electricity** <pause> **a swivel chair**

As you select words, you will notice that the Quick Correct window will appear, giving you alternatives to possible mistakes. This is a great way to correct mistakes. For example, let's say the word *discover* appears instead of the word *discovered* when you say the above sentence. If you say *Select* **discover**, you can correct the mistake quickly by saying *Choose* and the number that appears next to the correct word, as shown in Figure 1-17.

2. Your sentence should now read, *Thomas Jefferson invented a swivel chair.* It is easier for speech recognition software to select groups of words or phrases than individual words. Clear the screen and try this:

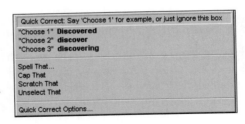

figure 1-17

Use the **Quick Correct** Window to Correct Mistakes You May Have Made

Benjamin Franklin wrote a famous book.

Select **Benjamin Franklin** <pause> **Thomas Jefferson**

Select **a famous book** <pause> **the Declaration of Independence**

3. Your sentence should now read, *Thomas Jefferson wrote the Declaration of Independence.*

3b

☑️ **Double-check** your NaturallySpeaking reference card if you need to review the substitution routine.

C Deselect Words and Use *Resume With*

At times you'll select the wrong word and you will wish to unselect it. Other times you will wish to use the selecting technique to position the insertion point with your voice. Another command, *Resume With*, completely erases everything following your insertion point and lets you start dictating again from a selected portion of the text. You can do all of these things with the following commands:

- *Move Right/Left 1 (Character)*
- *Unselect That*
- *Resume With*

1. Clear the screen and try this:

Neil Armstrong was the first person on the moon.

Select **Neil Armstrong** <pause> *Move Right 1 Character*

Select **first person** <pause> *Move Left 1 Character*

Select **on the moon** <pause> *Unselect That*

Select **Neil Armstrong** <pause> *Unselect That*

2. The *Resume With* command is a powerful way to erase part of a sentence and begin again. Clear the screen and try this:

Neil Armstrong was the first person on the moon.

Resume With **Neil Armstrong** <pause>

was a great astronaut.

3. Try dictating the following list of cities; then practice your substituting, deselecting, and inserting techniques. Clear your screen before you start.

I want to visit the following North American locations:

Seattle!
Toronto!
San Francisco!

Select **North American** <pause> **European**

Select **Seattle** <pause> **London**

Select **Toronto** <pause> **Madrid**

Select **San Francisco** <pause> **Moscow**

Select **London** <pause> *Move Left 1 (Character)* <pause> **Exciting**

Select **Madrid** <pause> *Move Left 1 (Character)* <pause> **Romantic**

Select **Moscow** <pause> *Move Left 1 (Character)* <pause> **Mysterious**

3c

☑ Double-check your NaturallySpeaking reference card if you need to review how to unselect or deselect words.

D Select and Delete Errors

Sometimes you'll want to remove a specific word or phrase rather than deleting an entire block of text. To do this, use the *Delete* command:

- *Delete That*

1. Clear your screen and try the following sentence while practicing deleting and inserting words and phrases:

The tall woman went to Chicago for a business lunch.

Select **lunch** <pause> *Delete That*

Select **for a business** <pause> *Delete That*

Select **Chicago** <pause> *Delete That*

Orlando on vacation

F Y I Your sentence should now read, *The tall woman went to Orlando on vacation.*

3d

☑ Double-check your NaturallySpeaking reference card if you forget how to use the delete option.

E Select Again

Sometimes a word or punctuation mark will appear several times in the same paragraph or on the same page. When you try to select a frequently used word like *the*, NaturallySpeaking may choose the wrong instance of the word. There are several different techniques you can use to get to the right word in your document:

- *Select Again*
- *Select <word>*
- *Select <several words>* (or a phrase adjacent to the word you wish to select)
- Select the word with your mouse

1. Try this paragraph:

I want to visit several countries, including: France, Germany, England, and Spain. I want to visit several famous cities. I want to take many things: my airline tickets, my passport, my money, and my bags.

2. Correct any errors, then select certain words again and again. Try this:

Select **my**
Select **my**
Select Again
Select Again
(Say *Select Again* until you have selected each *my* in the document several times.)

Select **I want to**
Select **I want to**
Select Again
Select Again
(Say *Select Again* until you have selected each *I want to* several times.)

┌─ **F Y I** ─┐ Notice that NaturallySpeaking selects words starting at the bottom of the page and moves up the page selection by selection.

3. Don't forget that your mouse still works! Try deleting words and punctuation with your mouse and voice together, like this:

(Select **France,** with your mouse)
Delete That

(Select **my money,** with your mouse)
Delete That

(Select **several famous cities,** with your mouse)
Delete That

(Select **including:** with your mouse)
Delete That

4. Select and replace every instance of **I want to** with **I need to**.

3e

Double-check your NaturallySpeaking reference card if you forget these selection options.

F Spell Web and Email Addresses and the Alphabet

From time to time you will need to spell a word letter by letter or part by part for NaturallySpeaking instead of saying the word normally. Two good examples are web and email addresses. NaturallySpeaking will guess that you're attempting to spell a web or email address; all you have to do is spell it normally. For example, say the following:

No Caps On **http w w w** *Dot* **disney** *Dot* **com** *No Caps Off* = http://www.disney.com

No Caps On **w w w** *Dot* **yahoo** *Dot* **com** *No Caps Off* = www.yahoo.com

No Caps On **miller at speaking about** *Dot* **com** *No Caps Off* = miller@speakingabout.com

You will need to know the following commands as you proceed:

- *No Caps On* will prevent letters from being capitalized.
- *No Caps Off* will allow letters to be capitalized again.
- *http* will signal to NaturallySpeaking that this is a web address. The *://* punctuation marks will be added automatically.
- *www* will also signal to NaturallySpeaking that this is a web address. The *http://* phrase won't be added.
- *Dot* creates a period in web addresses.
- Say *Press* **a**, *Press* **b**, *Press* **c**, and so on to spell the letters of the alphabet.
- *Say (Press) Backspace to delete a letter.*

Let's start by spelling the alphabet:

1. NaturallySpeaking provides an easy way to spell letter by letter. Say the alphabet using the *Press* command before you say each letter:

   Press **a**
   Press **b**
   Press **c**
   Press **d**
   (Continue speaking until you say the entire alphabet, ending with *Press* **z**)

2. If a letter gives you any trouble (for example, an *8* appears instead of the letter *a*), try spelling with the military or phonetic alphabet instead of your A, B, C's. For example, **Alpha** = *a*; **Bravo** = *b*; **Charlie** = *c*.

   Say the alphabet again, substituting these words instead of saying the letters. Say *Press* before saying each word, as in *Press* **Alpha**:

   Say *Press* followed by . . .

Alpha	**Bravo**	**Charlie**	**Delta**	**Echo**	**Foxtrot**
Golf	**Hotel**	**India**	**Juliet**	**Kilo**	**Lima**
Mike	**November**	**Oscar**	**Papa**	**Quebec**	**Romeo**
Sierra	**Tango**	**Uniform**	**Victor**	**Whiskey**	**X ray**
Yankee	**Zulu**				

3. Review the first example below the introductory paragraph on page 1-26. Now clear the screen
and try the following web addresses starting with **http**. Say the letters individually, such as **a b
c**, **c b s** , or **n b c**:

http://www.**abc.com**
http://www.**cbs.com**
http://www.**nbc.com**

4. Review the second example below the introductory paragraph on page 1-26 and create the
following web addresses without the *http://*:

www.**speakingabout.com**
www.**yahoo.com**
www.**disney.com**

5. Review the third example on page 1-26 and create the following email addresses:

miller@speakingabout.com
michael@disney.com
steve@aol.com

6. If an email or web address is not composed of commonly used words or phrases, you will need
to spell it letter by letter. Try the following examples using the *Press* command, such as *Press* **m**
<pause> *Press* **k** <pause> *Press* **i** <pause> *Press* **m** to spell out *mkim*. Use the *Press Shift 2*
command to create the @. Try these:

mkim@corpview.com
www.corpview.com
abcdefg@swep.com

3f

✓ **Double-check** your NaturallySpeaking reference card if you forget how to spell words
letter by letter or part by part.

G Transfer Your NaturallySpeaking Skills to Microsoft Word or Corel WordPerfect

If you have the *Standard*, *Preferred*, or a higher version of NaturallySpeaking and you also have
Word or WordPerfect on your computer, review the following skills to transfer your speech abilities
to Word or WordPerfect:

1. Close DragonPad and any other open applications and turn on your microphone by clicking the
Microphone On/Off button.

2. Open Word or WordPerfect by saying *Start Microsoft Word* (*Start WordPerfect*), or open one
of these programs with your mouse.

3. Try some of the exercises you have previously completed in this activity using Word or WordPerfect instead of DragonPad:

- Try the **Scratch That** and **Undo That** commands found in Part A (*Scratch or Undo Errors Immediately*).

- Select and substitute words as shown in Part B (*Substitute Words*).

- Select and unselect words as shown in Part C (*Deselect Words and Use Resume With*).

- Practice selecting and deleting errors in Word or WordPerfect by reviewing Part D (*Select and Delete Errors*).

- Practice selecting multiple words in a paragraph using the commands found in Part E (*Select Again*).

- Try spelling web addresses in your word processor as you did in Part F (*Spell Web and Email Addresses and the Alphabet*).

4. Close Word or WordPerfect by saying *(Click) File, Exit*.

Lesson 4 | *Training Speech Errors Permanently*

OBJECTIVES In this lesson you will …

(A) Train New Words by Spelling Them

(B) Train Words with the *Correction* Window

(C) Train Names with the *Add Individual Word* Feature

(D) Learn to Use the *Quick Correct* List Alternatives

(E) Transfer Your Correction Dialog Skills to Microsoft Word or Corel WordPerfect

Speaking About . . . Proofreading and Editing

In Lesson 3 you quickly corrected simple mistakes using the "select and replace" method. This method allows you to easily replace one word with another, but it has one drawback—it doesn't improve your recognition accuracy. What do you do if a mistake keeps recurring, or if you wish to say a word that NaturallySpeaking doesn't have in its vocabulary?

To fix nagging errors permanently and to improve your recognition accuracy, *YOU MUST TRAIN your software to understand you!* The more you train incorrect words, the smarter your software will become. You will learn a variety of training and accuracy-building techniques in this lesson.

After you start correcting errors and training new words, it is extremely important that you exit NaturallySpeaking in the proper fashion. As you exit, be sure to save changes to your personal voice profile by saying *Yes* or *Click Yes* as prompted in the **Save Changes?** prompt box shown in Figure 1-18. Otherwise, the words you have corrected or added to your personal voice profile will not be saved and the same mistakes will recur from session to session.

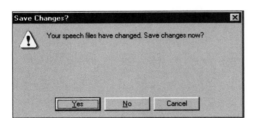

figure 1-18

As You Exit, Save Changes to Your Speech Files

(A) Train New Words by Spelling Them

If you train new and unique words consistently, you will see your recognition accuracy get better and better. If you don't add new words and correct mistakes, your accuracy will remain at the same level—never improving.

A very quick way to add new words to your user profile is with the *Spell* command. With Dragon NaturallySpeaking you can spell new words by saying them normally (**a**, **b**, **c**, **d**, and so forth), or you can use the military alphabet and the *Press* command as explained in Lesson 3, Part F.

Remember that saying the word *Click* is optional. Say *Click* if NaturallySpeaking doesn't seem to understand your command. In this lesson you will say the names of many buttons found in windows. For example, to press the **Record** button with your voice, you can say either *Click Record* or just *Record.*. To signal that a word or command is optional, it is shown in parentheses: *(Click)*

1. Open **DragonPad** and turn on your microphone.

2. Corporate View is a simulated corporation with many unique strategic business unit names. Each name is spelled with two capitalized words without a space between them, such as *PublishView*, *TeleView*, and *MediView*. You will train the first of these names. To open the **Correction** window (see Figure 1-19), say:

Spell

3. After the **Correction** window opens, immediately begin spelling. Remember to use the *Cap* command for capital letters.

Cap **P u b l i s h** *Cap* **V i e w**

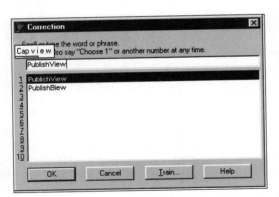

figure 1-19

Train New Words Using the Spell Technique

4. To get ready to record your new word, say:

(Click) Train

5. Record the new word so NaturallySpeaking will understand the word *PublishView* when you say it in the future. Say:

(Click) Record

Say **PublishView** as clearly as you can (as shown in Figure 1-20).

(Click) Done

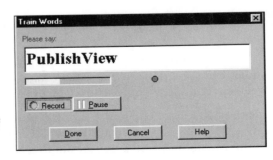

figure 1-20

Record Your Pronunciation of the New Word

6. Close the *Correction* window with the following command. Say:

(Click) OK

7. Say the name a couple of times to see if it recorded correctly. If *PublishView* does not appear with the correct spelling, repeat Steps 2-6.

PublishView   PublishView

8. Repeat Steps 2-6 while training these additional unique SBU names from Corporate View. Use the military or phonetic alphabet to help you if incorrect letters appear. Don't forget to say or click *Backspace* to delete mistakes.

MediView = ***Spell Cap*** M e d i ***Cap*** V i e w

TeleView = ***Spell Cap*** T e l e ***Cap*** V i e w

9. Say the following sentence and see if all three new names appear correctly:

The names of the three major business units are PublishView, MediView, and TeleView.

┌─ **F Y I** ┐   If you train words using capital letters, as in these examples, the words will appear with capital letters when you say them. If you don't want certain words to appear with capital letters, train them with lowercase letters only.

10. Clear your screen before continuing to the next exercise.

4a

Double-check Section 4a of your NaturallySpeaking reference card if you forget how to spell and record new words.

B Train Words with the *Correction* Window

Understanding human speech with all of our many accents is very difficult for a computer. Computers make mistakes—lots of them—so they must be trained. The *Correction* window is an important key to improving your recognition accuracy. Use this box to train your system to understand you better.

You will need to use the following commands to improve your recognition accuracy:

- Say *Select <the incorrect word(s)>*; then say *Spell That* or *Correct That*; then spell the word(s) letter by letter.

- Say *Backspace* to delete a letter.

- Use the *Cap* or *Caps On/Off* command for capital letters.

- Say *(Click) Train* or choose the **Train** button to open the **Train Words** window; then say *(Click) Record* or choose the **Record** button to record the word; then say *(Click) Done*; then say *(Click) OK* to continue dictating.

You can turn the capitalization mode on, then off again with the *Caps On/Off* option. This is particularly helpful if you have a long series of words that need to be capitalized, such as in a title.

1. Open **DragonPad** and click on your microphone.

2. The television program "Star Trek" was full of words that are not used by mortals of our generation: words like *Klingon, tricorder, Cardassian, Romulan,* and *trilithium.* Try training the word *trilithium,* which is pronounced **try lith e um.** (Trilithium is a fictional crystal used to create interstellar explosives.) Say:

trilithium

3. Your computer probably came up with *try lithium* or something equally wrong. Say this:

***Select* <try lithium>** (or whatever appears in the place of *trilithium*)

4. See Figure 1-21. Notice that the correct word does not appear in the Quick Correct list, so you must correct it in a different way. Display the **Correction** window by saying either:

Spell That or *Correct That*

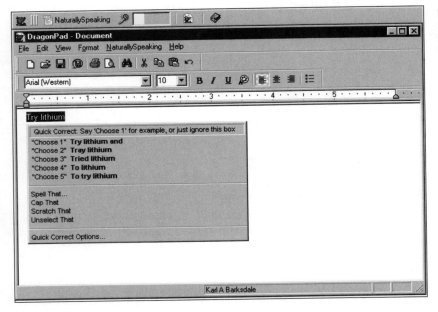

figure 1-21

Select the Incorrect Word

5. As shown in Figure 1-22, spell out the correct word letter by letter (say *Backspace* to delete mistakes):

t r i l i t h i u m

6. Say *(Click) Train* or choose the **Train** button with your mouse.

7. When the **Train Words** window appears, say:

(Click) Record (or choose the **Record** button with your mouse)

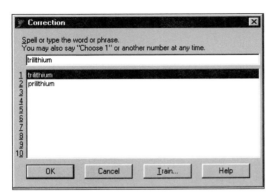

figure 1-22

Spell Out the Correct
Word

8. Say the new word clearly, as shown in Figure 1-23:

trilithium

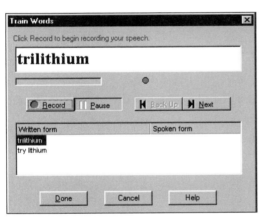

figure 1-23

The Train Words
Window

9. Record the incorrect word that appeared as *try lithium*, as shown in Figure 1-24. For example, say:

try <pause> **lithium**

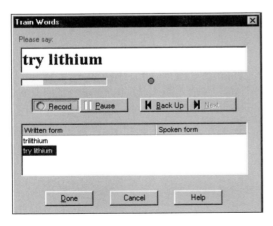

figure 1-24

Record **try** <pause> **lithium**

10. To close the *Train Words* window, say:

(Click) Done (or choose **Done** with your mouse)

11. To close the *Correction* window, say:

(Click) OK (or choose **OK** with your mouse)

12. Repeat the word a couple of times to see if it trained correctly. If *trilithium* doesn't appear correctly when you say it, try training it again by repeating Steps 2-11.

trilithium   trilithium

13. Train the following interplanetary cultures and terms from "Star Trek." . Use the *Cap* command in order to capitalize the first letter of some of these names:

Cardassian	=	(say *Cap* **C a r d a s s i a n**)
Klingon	=	(say *Cap* **K l i n g o n**)
Romulan	=	(say *Cap* **R o m u l a n**)

F Y I   Klingons (pronounced **cling ons**) are a warrior race from their "home world" of Qo'nos. Cardassians and Romulans live outside of the Federation's neutral zone.

14. After you have trained several of these interstellar names and terms, say the following sentence. How is your accuracy on the words you have trained?

The Klingon took the trilithium crystals from the Cardassian leader and smuggled the crystals across the Romulan neutral zone.

15. Clear your screen before continuing to the next exercise.

4b

Double-check your NaturallySpeaking reference card if you forget how to train new words.

C Train Names with the *Add Individual Word* Feature

Sometimes you may want to train a word, a phrase, or a name that you use frequently. Most names are not part of the Dragon NaturallySpeaking vocabulary. An easy way to train names is with the *Add IndividualWord* feature. These are the steps you need to follow:

- Say **(Click) NaturallySpeaking**, **Words**, **Add Individual Word**
- Spell the name, word, or phrase letter by letter.
- Say **Space Bar** to create a space.
- Say **Backspace** to delete a letter.

- Use the *Cap* command for capital letters.
- Say *(Click) Add* or choose the **Add** button to train a word.
- Say *(Click) Record* or choose the **Record** button to record a word.
- Record the new word, phrase, or name and say *(Click) Done*.

1. You will train your own name using the following steps. In our sample, we are training the name *Sojourner Truth*, the nickname of the famous 19th-century abolitionist. Substitute your name for her name throughout this exercise. To open the **Add Individual Word** window (Figure 1-25), say:

(Click) NaturallySpeaking

Words

Add Individual Word

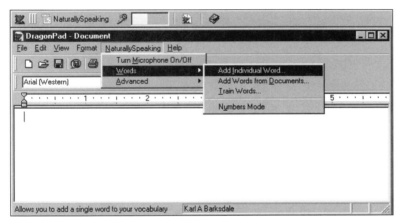

figure 1-25

Open the **Add Individual Word** Window

2. Now spell your name, as shown in Figure 1-26. Use the *Space Bar* command to create a space:

S o j o u r n e r *Space Bar* **T r u t h**

(Click) Add   (**NOTE:** Make sure the **I want to train the pronunciation of this word** box remains checked.)

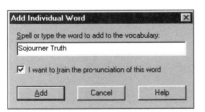

figure 1-26

Spell the Name and Select **Add**

3. Record your name. Use the following commands to help you. Say:

(Click) Record

Say your name clearly, as shown in Figure 1-27: **Sojourner Truth**

(Click) Done

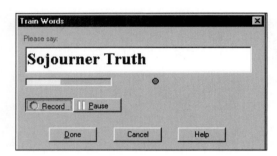

figure 1-27

Record Your Name as
Shown in This Example

4. Try saying your name several more times to see if it has been trained properly. Repeat Steps 1-3 to train your name again if it comes up wrong:

Sojourner Truth Sojourner Truth

5. Repeat Steps 1-4 again, training the names of five of your family members and friends.

6. Clear your screen before continuing to the next exercise.

4c

☑ Double-check your NaturallySpeaking reference card if you forget how to train names and other words and phrases.

Ⓓ Learn to Use the *Quick Correct* List Alternatives

The easiest way to improve your recognition accuracy is to choose correct words from the *Quick Correct* list. This feature works best in DragonPad, and it isn't always available in other applications. Here's how to get the most out of the *Quick Correct* list:

A. Speak in complete sentences.

B. Look for mistakes in your completed sentences.

C. Select every mistake, as shown in Figure 1-28, using the *Select* **<mistake>** command.

D. After the **Quick Correct** list opens, you have two alternatives:

Alternative 1. If the correct word appears in the **Quick Correct** list, use the *Choose* **<number>** command to choose it from the list, as shown in Figure 1-28. In this case, you would say *Choose 1* to replace the incorrect word *boxes* with the corrected word *box*.

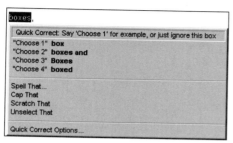

figure 1-28

Say **_Choose_** <**number**> to Select the Correct Numbered Word from the List

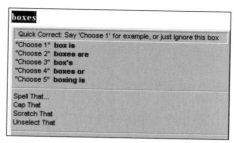

figure 1-29

Say **_Spell That_** to Spell and Record the Correct Word

Or

Alternative 2. If the correct word does *not* appear in the **Quick Correct** list, or if you feel the word needs to be trained permanently, use the **_Spell That_** command to open the **Correction** window. In Figure 1-29, the word *box* does not appear, so you need to use the **_Spell That_** command to spell and record the word.

 As the **Quick Correct** list opens, notice that you can also correct capitalization errors with the **_Cap That_** command, delete text with the **_Scratch That_** command, or deselect your text with the **_Unselect That_** command. (See Figure 1-29.)

E. Spell the word in the **Correction** window. If the word appears in the list as you are spelling, you have two alternatives:

Alternative 1. If the correct word appears in the Correction list as you spell, use the **_Choose_** <**number**> command to choose it from the list and return to your document.

Or

Alternative 2. If the correct word appears in your list, as shown in Figure 1-30, and you still wish to record the word, use the **_Select_** <**number**> command and say **_(Click) Train_**.

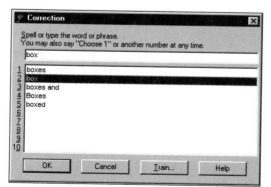

figure 1-30

Choose the Correct Word from the List

F. If you choose to record the word, say *(Click) Record*, record the correct word, record the incorrect word, and then say *(Click) Done*, *(Click) OK* to complete the recording process. (See Figure 1-31.)

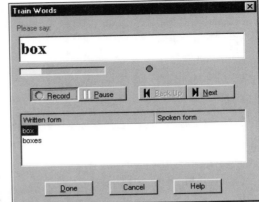

figure 1-31

Record the Words

1. Open **DragonPad** and dictate the following sentences. At the end of each sentence, look for errors and train every error that you may find, using the technique explained in this lesson:

There are many words that I don't understand.

After all, I am just a computer!

Sometimes I confuse the words and, at, and add.

What do you expect? Perfection?

To help me perform at my best, you must correct mistakes!

If the correct word appears in your Quick Correct list, an easy way to make the change is to pick, take, or choose the word from the list.

2. Dictate the entire paragraph below. See if your accuracy has improved as a result of your efforts in correcting your earlier mistakes:

There are many words that I don't understand. After all, I am just a computer! Sometimes I confuse the words and, at, and add. What do you expect? Perfection? To help me perform at my best, you must correct mistakes! If the correct word appears in your Quick Correct list, an easy way to make the change is to pick, take, or choose the word from the list.

3. Clear your screen before continuing to the next exercise.

4d

Double-check your NaturallySpeaking reference card if you forget how to choose correct words from the *Quick Correct* list.

Ⓔ Transfer Your Correction Dialog Skills to Microsoft Word or Corel WordPerfect

If you have the *Standard*, *Preferred*, or a higher version of NaturallySpeaking, and Word or WordPerfect is also installed properly on your computer, try this exercise using one of those powerful word processors. (**NOTE:** You can also complete this activity using DragonPad. The commands covered in this exercise work for all three programs.)

Use the following steps to correct your errors:

A. Speak in complete sentences.

B. Look for mistakes in your completed sentences.

C. Select every mistake, as shown in Figure 1-32, using the *Correct* **<mistake>** command.

D. After the **Correction** window opens, you have two alternatives:

Alternative 1. If the correct word appears in the **Correction** list, use the *Choose* **<number>** command to choose it from the list.

Or

Alternative 2. If the correct word does *not* appear immediately in the **Correction** list, spell the word out letter by letter. If the correct word appears while you are spelling, use the *Select* **<number>** command to avoid having to spell out the entire word.

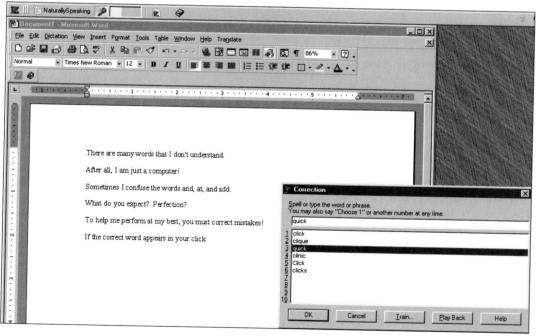

figure 1-32

Choose Correct Words from the Correction Window

E. If you chose Alternative 2 above, record the word in the **Train Words** window with the *(Click) Train*, then *(Click) Record* commands (see Figure 1-33).

Try using the *Correct* **<mistake>** command to train every mistake in the following exercise!

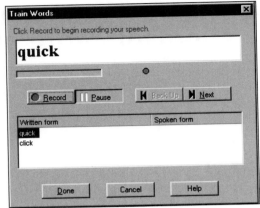

figure 1-33

Record the Word
That Is Giving You
Trouble

 If you accidentally make a selection with the *Select* **<mistake>** command, you can still choose an alternative from the **Correction** list and train the selection by saying *Correct That*. You can also correct an incorrect word instantly by saying *Correct That* immediately after you say the word.

1. Open Microsoft Word (or WordPerfect) by saying *Start Microsoft Word* (*Start WordPerfect*), or use DragonPad for this activity.

2. Speak the following dialog in complete sentences. At the end of each sentence, use the *Correct* **<mistake>** command to correct errors. If the correct alternative appears in your **Correction** list, say *Choose* **<number>**. If the correct word does not appear, spell the word letter by letter, say *(Click) Train*, and record the word:

As with people, messages have their own personalities.

Consider what personality best fits the needs of the audience before you begin writing.

Is the message scientific and objective, or is it entertaining and informative?

What is the tone, mood, feel, attitude, or voice of the message?

The personality and style of the message may add to or detract from the content of the message.

For example, a serious message written in an informal or humorous style may not receive the attention it deserves.

3. Train and correct any mistakes you may have made using the *Correct* **<mistake>** command.

4. Repeat this 100-word (500-character) dialogue. You can only make 10 mistakes to achieve 90 percent accuracy, 5 mistakes for 95 percent accuracy, and so on. However, by training your mistakes, you can push your accuracy level well over 95 percent! Speak clearly, and train and correct every mistake. Practice until you achieve a higher level of accuracy. **NOTE:** If you can say this dialogue in 60 seconds, your speed is over 100 words per minute.

As with people, messages have their own personalities. Consider what personality best fits the needs of the audience before you begin writing. Is the message scientific and objective, or is it entertaining and informative? What is the tone, mood, feel, attitude, or voice of the message? The personality and style of the message may add to or detract from the content of the message. For example, a serious message written in an informal or humorous style may not receive the attention it deserves.

5. Close Word, WordPerfect, or DragonPad by saying *(Click) File, Exit*. While exiting, save the document as **Personality**, and make sure you save changes to your speech profile.

4e

✔**Double-check** your NaturallySpeaking reference card if you forget how to correct words with the *Correct* **<mistake>** command.

Proofreading and Editing

An often-used phrase in corporate communication circles goes, "Great writers aren't born, they just proofread better than average writers." Great writing comes from great proofreading and editing of your first drafts. This is especially true with speech recognition writers.

Old-fashioned typists had an advantage in that they could actually feel mistakes with their hands as they typed. Today, computer users must proofread a document carefully and see the mistakes visually.

In this practice exercise, you will dictate the text, proofread it, and then train all your errors using the *Quick Correct* or *Correction* windows until you achieve nearly 100 percent accuracy. Then you will take a speed and accuracy test. Good luck!

1. Open a new document, turn your microphone on, and read aloud the following excerpt from *Century 21 Keyboarding & Information Processing, Sixth Edition* (p. 73), which we call "Speaking of Success." There are some tongue twisters in the paragraph. For instance, the phrase *in power, in fame, and in income* needs to be dictated and even trained very carefully.

Speaking of success.

Success does not mean the same thing to everyone. For some, it means to get to the top at all costs: in power, in fame, and in income. For others, it means just to fulfill their basic needs or wants with as little effort as required.

New Paragraph

Go to Sleep

2. Proofread the paragraph carefully. Select and train any words that are incorrect as you learned to do in this lesson.

F Y I If a word like *Fathers* appears at the start of the third sentence instead of the phrase *For others*, say **Correct** Fathers, then train the phrase *For others*.

3. Try the next paragraph of the excerpt:

Wake Up

Most people fall within the two extremes. They work quite hard to better their lives at home, at school, and in the social world. They realize that success for them is not in being at the top, but rather in trying to improve their quality of life.

New Paragraph

Go To Sleep

F Y I Before you proofread, remember to say *Go to Sleep* or "park" your insertion point in a blank space on the screen so that if breathing errors occur, you can spot them easily and delete them.

4. Proofread for errors and train all the words you missed.

5. Delete all of your previous sentences and start with a clean document window. Dictate both paragraphs together:

Wake Up

Speaking of success.

Success does not mean the same thing to everyone. For some, it means to get to the top at all costs: in power, in fame, and in income. For others, it means just to fulfill their basic needs or wants with as little effort as required.

Most people fall within the two extremes. They work quite hard to better their lives at home, at school, and in the social world. They realize that success for them is not in being at the top, but rather in trying to improve their quality of life.

Go to Sleep

6. Proofread your document, looking for any picky little words that are still giving you trouble, then correct and train the errors.

7. Try dictating the paragraph again while timing yourself! There are over 500 characters. If you can say this paragraph in less than 60 seconds, your speed is over 100 words per minute! More important, how many mistakes will you make? To get a rough idea of your accuracy, take the total number of mistakes you made and subtract this number from 100. Before you start, delete all of your previous sentences so you can start dictating with a clean document window.

8. Save your work as **Success**.

section 2

Speech-Writing and Formatting Solutions

By now you have learned the essentials of NaturallySpeaking and your accuracy is improving with every passing session. It's now time to face some new challenges unique to speech recognition users.

Thankfully, some problems have nearly disappeared. Take spelling, for instance. NaturallySpeaking can only display the words in its extensive vocabulary—and they are all spelled correctly. Only *you* can introduce spelling errors. When you train a word, make sure you spell it correctly, or your incorrect spelling will be added to your personal vocabulary list and the word will appear incorrectly every time you say it.

While misspelling words is a minuscule problem, misusing words is commonplace. Some speech errors are hard to catch. There's the obvious problem of homonyms, words that sound the same but are spelled differently and have different meanings. Take *to*, *too*, and *two*, for example. NaturallySpeaking must guess by the context of the sentence which word to display.

Other writing essentials must also be applied, like the rules of capitalization and the appropriate use of all those funny-looking characters such as the following: ~, @, #, $, %, &, *, [,], {, }, (, and). Before a document can be printed, it must also be formatted with appropriate structure and headings. You may choose to do some of your formatting with your mouse and keyboard, but much of it can be completed more efficiently with your voice.

There are a lot of writing and formatting issues to talk about, so let's start speaking again.

Lesson 5 | *Correcting Capitalization*

OBJECTIVES In this lesson you will ...

(A) Capitalize Text

(B) Uppercase Text

(C) Lowercase Text

(D) Capitalize and Compound Words

Speaking About . . . Capitalization

NaturallySpeaking will normally capitalize the first word of each sentence, but often it won't know exactly which other words you want capitalized. It's up to you to take charge and order it to capitalize properly.

In this lesson we will work on the mechanics of capitalization. In the *Speaking About . . . Capitalization* activity we will work in more detail on when, and when not, to use capitalization in your writing.

F Y I Here's a little trick that will come in handy: If you hold down the **Shift** key while speaking, NaturallySpeaking can interpret what you speak only as words, not commands. (You can then say words like **select** or **correct** without causing all sorts of problems.) However, when you hold down the **Ctrl** key while speaking, NaturallySpeaking can interpret what you speak only as commands. If you're having trouble with a command like *Cap That*, hold down the **Ctrl** key while speaking the command, and NaturallySpeaking will force the command to work.

Capitalize Text

There are several options that you can use when capitalizing. You can select the word and say *Cap That*, or you can turn the capitalize mode on and off and capitalize multiple words as you say them. The capitalization commands you will need are as follows:

- *Cap*
- *Cap That* or *Capitalize That*
- *Caps On/Off*

1. Clear your screen and dictate the following sentence, then correct the capitalization problems using the selection method, as shown:

Mary attended the marine wildlife institute.

Select **marine wildlife institute** <pause> *Cap That*

2. Clear your screen. Try turning the capitalize mode on before you begin dictating. After you finish capitalizing, don't forget to turn the capitalize mode off to go back to your normal dictation mode.

Caps On

The Alpine Country Club Official Membership List

Caps Off

> **F Y I** It helps to say the *Caps On* command almost as one word: Say *CapsOn,* not *Caps* <pause> *On*. Watch the **Results Box** in NaturallySpeaking to see if the capitalize mode has been turned on or off properly. Sometimes the system gets stuck in *Caps On* mode. The Results Box will help you detect whether you have turned capitalization off by displaying the *Caps Off* command.

3. Clear your screen. Capitalizing individual words as you come to them is easy using the *Cap* command. You can also capitalize a word immediately after saying it with the *Cap That* command. Try capitalizing the title of this fictitious legal magazine using several methods:

The *Cap* **National** *Cap* **Legal** *Cap* **Review**

The national <pause> *Cap That* **legal** <pause> *Cap That* **review** <pause> *Cap That*

The national legal review <pause> *Cap That*

4. NaturallySpeaking provides a variety of ways for you to say capitalization commands. For instance, you can substitute the *Cap That* command with *Capitalize That*. You can also select text and say *Format That Capitals, Format That Initial Caps, Format That Cap,* or *Format That Caps*. All of these options are legal commands in NaturallySpeaking. Repeat Steps 1, 2, and 3 substituting these alternatives for the traditional *Cap* and *Cap That* commands.

> **5a**
> **Double-check** your NaturallySpeaking reference card if you forget the capitalization commands.

B Uppercase Text

Words entirely in UPPERCASE are often used in titles. Uppercased words are also used to indicate shouting in email messages. You can select the word and say *All Caps That*, uppercase a single word before you come to it, or turn the uppercase mode on and off to uppercase multiple words as you say them. Here are the uppercase commands:

- *All Caps*
- *All Caps That*
- *All Caps On/Off*

1. Clear your screen and dictate the following book title, uppercasing the title after the fact:

Treasure Island

Select **Treasure Island** <pause> *All Caps That*

2. Your title should now appear as *TREASURE ISLAND*. Clear your screen. Uppercase the following headline from December 7, 1941, with the *All Caps On/Off* method:

All Caps On

Japan attacked Pearl Harbor early this morning

All Caps Off

> **F Y I** Watch the **Results Box** to see if the uppercase mode has been turned on or off properly. It helps to say the *All Caps On* command almost as one word. Say *AllCapsOn*, not *All* <pause> *Caps* <pause> *On.*

3. You can uppercase a single word as you speak, or several words after you have said them. Try this exercise:

All Caps **Toy** <slight pause> *All Caps* **Story**

Treasure Island <slight pause> *All Caps That*

4. NaturallySpeaking provides alternatives for the *All Caps* commands. You can select text and say *Format That All Caps* or *Format That Uppercase*. Repeat Steps 1, 2, and 3, substituting these alternatives for the traditional *All Caps That* command.

`5b`

✓**Double-check** your NaturallySpeaking reference card if you forget the uppercase commands!

ⓒ Lowercase Text

Sometimes words become capitalized that shouldn't be. You can select the capitalization error and say *No Caps That* to fix the mistake. You can also *No Caps* a single word before you come to it, or turn the *No Caps* mode on and off as you need to. The lowercase commands are as follows:

- *No Caps*
- *No Caps That*
- *No Caps On/Off*

1. Clear your screen and dictate the following book title, altering the capitalization using the selection method:

Treasure Island

Select **Treasure Island** <pause> *All Caps That*

Select **Treasure Island** <pause> *No Caps That*

2. Clear your screen. Use the *No Caps On/Off* mode, then practice adding the capitalization later:

No Caps On

president george washington marched into pennsylvania.

No Caps Off

Select **president george washington**

Cap That

Select **pennsylvania**

Cap That

F Y I   It helps to say the *No Caps On* command almost as one word: Say *NoCapsOn*, not *No* <pause> *Caps* <pause> *On*. Watch the **Results Box** to view whether the uppercase mode has been turned on or off properly.

---

3. NaturallySpeaking has alternatives for *No Caps That*. You can select text and say *Format That No Caps* or *Format That Lowercase*. Repeat Steps 1 and 2, substituting these alternatives for the traditional *No Caps That* commands.

Double-check your NaturallySpeaking reference card if you forget the **No Caps That** commands.

       5c

D Capitalize and Compound Words

Sometimes you may need to put words together that normally would be two separate words. This is called compounding. NaturallySpeaking uses a simple command, *Compound That*, to accomplish this task. In this exercise, you will capitalize and compound a few of the fictitious Corporate View strategic business unit names:

1. Clear your screen and dictate the following business unit name. Correct the capitalization before compounding the two words:

travel view

Select **travel view** <pause> *Cap That*

Select **Travel View** <pause> *Compound That*

2. *TravelView* should appear on your screen. Now try a few more business names, but this time, watch how NaturallySpeaking allows commands like *Compound That* to work on the word next to the insertion point. Once again, correct the capitalization before compounding the words:

Money view	**Retail view**
Cap That	*Cap That*
Compound That	*Compound That*

Double-check your NaturallySpeaking reference card if you need to review the compound words command.

Speaking About...

Capitalization

Speaking Solutions in This Lesson . . .

A. Capitalize the First Word of Every Sentence

B. Capitalize the Days of the Week, Names of Months, and Holidays

C. Capitalize Important Words in a Title

D. Capitalize Proper Nouns and Proper Adjectives

E. Capitalize Titles Before a Person's Name

F. Leave the Seasons in Lowercase Letters

G. Capitalize Directions If They Stand for a Specific Place

Mastering capitalization isn't difficult. Many capitalization errors are made through carelessness—a simple proofing will correct most of the difficulties.

Review the rules for capitalization in the following exercises.

> **F Y I** Don't train words using capital letters unless the word is always capitalized. For example, the words *animal* and *farm* in the book title *Animal Farm* shouldn't be individually trained with capital letters because the words mostly appear as lowercase letters in other contexts.

A. Capitalize the First Word of Every Sentence

1. Clear your screen. Capitalize the first word of every sentence. Normally your speech software will take care of this automatically! All you need to do is say the sentences. Try saying this:

This is the first time he has used a snowboard.

Speech recognition software is better than ever.

2. Correct and train any errors and repeat the sentences.

B. Capitalize the Days of the Week, Names of Months, and Holidays

1. Capitalize the days of the week, names of months, and holidays. Let your software try and get it right the first time you say it. If it doesn't, you can correct the capitalization errors later. Try this:

He spoke on Monday and Tuesday.

During December and June she received her bonus checks.

On Memorial Day and Independence Day he took a break; during Thanksgiving and Labor Day, he relaxed.

2. Correct and train any mistakes and repeat the sentences.

C. Capitalize Important Words in a Title

1. Capitalize important words in a title (including the beginning and ending words).

Harry Potter and the Sorcerer's Stone

Fishing for the Complete Idiot

Animal Farm

2. Correct and train errors and repeat each sentence.

D. Capitalize Proper Nouns and Proper Adjectives

1. Capitalize proper nouns and proper adjectives such as nationalities, languages, geographic places, groups of people, and formal periods of time.

I studied history, French, math, and English in school.

The British and the Russians enjoyed studying about the Renaissance.

Three Japanese students took my class.

A boy from Arkansas got the lead in the new Spielberg movie.

2. Correct and train your mistakes and repeat the sentences.

E. Capitalize Titles Before a Person's Name

1. Capitalize a title that takes the place of a person's name unless the title is preceded by the word *my* (or another possessive pronoun like *their, our, his, her, your*). Try to capitalize these sentences correctly:

President Jones was here.

Senator Miller walked in.

Professor Johnson lectured.

"Come, Mother, let's go."

"Hey, Dad, let's eat."

2. Leave these lowercase. Try these sentences:

The president was here.

The senator walked in.

The professor lectured.

My mother is here.

My dad is hungry.

3. Correct and train errors and repeat the sentences.

F. Leave the Seasons in Lowercase Letters

1. Do not capitalize the seasons. Try these examples:

I love winter and fall.

I don't like spring and summer.

I love Paris in the spring.

2. Train and correct your errors and repeat the sentences.

G. Capitalize Directions If They Stand for a Specific Place

1. Only capitalize directions (north, south, east, west) if they stand for a specific place. Try these sentences:

When I'm lost in the North Woods, I always go east.

The wind is blowing from the east.

I used to live in the East.

2. Correct and train your errors and repeat the sentences.

3. Save your work using **Capital** as your file name.

Think Before You Speak . . .

Read these sentences in your mind, determining where capitalization should be placed, and then try each sentence. Add these sentences to your **Capital** file and resave your file. Correct the mistakes. You may need to train some words, names and phrases as you go along.

my dad and I always hike the north face of the mountain.

i turned to president truman and shook his hand.

he played cowboys and indians all day long.

my mom's favorite song is "i heard it through the grapevine."

stop, dad!

the director of *guys and dolls* is coming to dinner.

jane austen wrote during the romantic period of literature.

i have science with professor miller.

i've always loved living in the west near the rockies.

he married a hawaiian native.

Double-check your answers on the Web at www.speakingabout.com. Click the **Speaking About . . . NaturallySpeaking** link and select **Speaking About . . . Answers**.

Lesson 6

Creating Symbols and Special Characters

OBJECTIVES   In this lesson you will . . .

(A) Say All of the Funny Characters

(B) Create Voice Emoticons

Speaking About . . . Hyphens

You already know how to say punctuation marks. Commas, periods, exclamation marks, and question marks are easy. However, from time to time you will need to insert parentheses ( ) or use an ampersand (&) or an *at* sign (@). You may even need to use a tilde (~) or an asterisk (*) now and again.

A Say All of the Funny Characters

When keyboarding was the only vehicle that could be used for text entry, most people never knew the names of some of these more obscure symbols. They simply picked the symbols from the pictures on their keyboards. Learning the names of obscure characters like the open brace ({) or caret (^) will take a little extra work.

F Y I   If you have trouble saying any of these special characters, try training them! You can train them in the same way you learned to train words in Lesson 4.

1. Try saying each of the special characters and punctuation marks in Table 2-1 and see what symbols appear. Few people get them all correct the first time they try.

table 2-1   Saying Special Characters and Punctuation Marks

Symbol or Character	Say
'	Apostrophe, or Single Quote
'	Apostrophe
's	Apostrophe S
`	Back Quote
\	Back Slash
{	Open Brace, *or* Left Brace
}	Close Brace, *or* Right Brace
[	Open Bracket, *or* Left Bracket
]	Close Bracket, *or* Right Bracket
"	Open Quote, *or* Begin Quotes
"	Close Quote, *or* End Quotes
'	Open Single Quote, *or* Begin Single Quote
'	Close Single Quote, *or* End Single Quote
:	Colon
;	Semicolon
,	Comma
?	Question Mark
!	Exclamation Point, *or* Exclamation Mark
—	Dash *(NOTE: Your dash may appear as two hyphens: --.)*
.	Period, *or* Dot, *or* Point
...	Ellipsis
-	Hyphen
(	Open Paren, *or* Open Parenthesis, *or* Left Parenthesis
)	Close Paren, *or* Close Parenthesis, *or* Right Parenthesis
/	Slash, *or* Forward Slash
	Space Bar, *or* Press Space Bar *(This adds a blank space.)*
~	Tilde *(NOTE: If you have trouble, try saying Til-dah or Til-day.)*
@	At Sign

Symbol or Character	Say
$	Dollar Sign
€	Euro Sign
£	Pound Sterling Sign
©	Copyright Sign
™	Trademark Sign
®	Registered Sign
°	Degree Sign
^	Caret
#	Number Sign, *or* Pound Sign
*	Asterisk
%	Percent Sign
<	Open Angle Bracket, *or* Less Than
>	Close Angle Bracket, *or* Greater Than
&	Ampersand
_	Underscore
		Vertical Bar
+	Plus Sign
-	Minus Sign
=	Equals Sign, *or* Equals

2. Look up the following scrambled symbols in Table 2-1 or on your reference card and say them. Use the *Tab Key* command to place some space between each of the characters. Say:

& \ { } : " - ...

( ) / @ # * % # 's

< > [' _ | + - = ~

3. Try inserting special characters into the following paragraph. It sometimes helps to pause before and after you say a special character or punctuation mark.

Michael used a / in a sentence followed by a (and). Then he placed an & before an @. He # said, "An & spoke to an * last Friday." Then a ~ went _ and a + . Needless to say, this = /-}. & you later!

✓Double-check your NaturallySpeaking reference card if you need to review the special characters and punctuation marks.

B Create Voice Emoticons

Emoticons are symbols used in email to express emotion to readers. Creating emoticons is easy with special characters.

1. Practice using symbols by creating emoticons. Let's do the first one together and then you can figure out the rest:

Colon Hyphen Close Parenthesis

The end result should look like this happy face:

:-)

2. Create the following emoticons with some of the symbols and special characters from the list of commands in Table 2-1 or on your reference card. Next to each emoticon you will find the meaning of the image.

: - (	Sad
: - ()	Surprised
: - {	Scared
: - {)	Smile with a mustache
: - |	So-so
: - <	Very sad
; -)	Happy and winking
> :-(	Mad

3. NaturallySpeaking makes three of the most common emoticons easy to create. Say the following commands to create the emoticons shown below. (**NOTE:** If you have trouble making one of these emoticons, hold down the **Shift** key as you say the command.)

Smiley Face = :-)

Frowny Face = :-(

Winky Face = ;-)

Hyphens

Speaking Solutions in This Lesson . . .

A. Hyphenate Compound Words Beginning with *Self-*

B. Hyphenate Family Names

C. Use Hyphens to Connect Phrases Used as a Single Word

Use a hyphen to join words or groups of words or to note the division of a word at the end of a line. Voice Xpress may guess exactly where hyphens go, but sometimes it gets them wrong and you will need to make a correction.

A. Hyphenate Compound Words Beginning with *Self-*

1. Compound words beginning with *self-* will always use a hyphen. Say these hyphenated words (without saying the hyphen) and see if your software hyphenates them correctly. Correct any that come up incorrectly.

self-contained
self-pity
self-government

2. Some words beginning with *self-* are not hyphenated. If you aren't sure about the hyphen usage, you'll need to consult a dictionary. Try these words and see if your software leaves off the hyphen properly. Correct any that come up incorrectly.

selfish
selfsame
selfless

B. Hyphenate Family Names

Use a hyphen for family names:

father-in-law
mother-in-law
great-grandmother

C. Use Hyphens to Connect Several Words Used as a Phrase

Hyphens are used to show a connection between several words that are used as a phrase to express a single idea. Phrases that are always hyphenated include:

Forget-me-not
Matter-of-fact
Stick-in-the-mud
Stay-at-home
Up-to-date

Think Before You Speak . . .

Read the following sentences in your mind and determine where hyphens should be placed, then say each sentence without the hyphen(s). See how many Voice Xpress will correct on its own. Add any hyphens that your software misses. Save these sentences as **Hyphen**.

He asked his mother in law for money.

My father in law wanted a new sports car.

My motor home was self contained.

He was filled with self pity.

He believed in self support and self government.

With these simple words, "I do," I became a brother in law.

He made the purchase at the all in one store.

She left behind a forget me not gift.

Double-check your answers on the Web at **www.speakingabout.com**. Click the **Speaking About . . . NaturallySpeaking** link and select **Speaking About . . . Answers**.

Lesson 7 | *Generating Numbers*

OBJECTIVES In this lesson you will . . .

(A) Say Single Digits

(B) Say Double Digits and Beyond

(C) Say Decimals and Fractions

(D) Say Dates

(E) Say Phone Numbers

(F) Say Currency

(G) Say Times of Day

(H) Say Math Formulas

(I) Say Roman Numerals

(J) Create Numbered Lists

(K) Format Numbers as Text or Numerals

Speaking About . . . Numbers in Sentences

Dictating numbers can be complicated. There are dozens of formats and ways to use numbers. This lesson will take some work, but by the end of it you will be counting your new skills with all of your fingers and toes.

A Say Single Digits

1. Many times you can simply say the numbers 0 through 9. However, if the number is formatted incorrectly (for example, if *one* appears instead of *1*), use the ***Numeral* \<number\>** command to force a digit. Say ***Numeral 1*** to create a *1*. Try dictating these numbers:

0 1 2 3 4 5 6 7 8 9

2. If you wish to dictate many numbers, *without* saying the ***Numeral*** command, say:

Start Numbers Mode

0 1 2 3 4 5 6 7 8 9

Stop Numbers Mode

F Y I If you have difficulty dictating numbers, you can use the numbers mode. You can say either ***Start Numbers Mode*** or ***Numbers Mode On*** before you say the numbers, then say ***Stop Numbers Mode*** or ***Numbers Mode Off*** to go back to normal mode.

✓ **Double-check** your NaturallySpeaking reference card if you forget how to say the digits 0 through 9.

B Say Double Digits and Beyond

1. Say the following numbers the normal way. Place several spaces between each digit with the *Space Bar* or *Press Space Bar* command.

10	11	12	13	14	15	16	17	18	19	20
22	37	46	54	61	73	84	99			
100	200	300	400	500	600	700	800	900		
126	298	365	423	590	688	791	842	999		

10,786   49,873   77,777   89,712

147,894   598,809   923,557

1,789,645   6,437,835   8,976,764

✓ **Double-check** your NaturallySpeaking reference card if you need to review how to say the numbers 10 and above.

C Say Decimals and Fractions

1. Try the following numbers. For the period, say *Point*, as in **five** *Point* **six**. (Place two spaces between each set of numbers.)

5.6   6.98   3.7   1.2   3.65

2.2   8.543   6.5   3.3   7.9

2. You can say fractions in one of two ways: You can say them normally, for example, **one half, one fourth,** and **five sixteenths**. Or you can use *Slash* (/) as in **1** *Slash* **2**. Say the first line of fractions below naturally, and then use the slash method in the second line. Place two spaces between each fraction.

1/2   1/4   1/5   5/8   5/16   9/10

1/2   1/4   1/5   5/8   5/16   9/10

✓ **Double-check** your NaturallySpeaking reference card if you forget how to say decimals and fractions.

D Say Dates

1. You can say dates using regular numbers and the *Comma* command. Say:

July four *Comma* seventeen seventy-six

Now try these:

July 14, 1805
March 30, 1984
August 5, 1987
January 1, 2000
June 14, 2005

2. You can also say dates in numeric format with the *Slash* command. For example, **oh three *Slash* twelve *Slash* fifty four**, or **twelve *Slash* five *Slash* ninety-nine**. Try these:

03/12/54
12/5/99
1/14/00
3/30/11

7d

✔ **Double-check** your NaturallySpeaking reference card if you forget how to say dates.

E Say Phone Numbers

1. Try the following phone numbers. Say the numbers naturally, pausing slightly where the hyphens go, but don't say the hyphens. However, you will need to say the parentheses. For example, for the last number, say **one *Open Paren* seven six five *Close Paren* five five five oh one seven one.**

555-0112
555-0182
765-555-0171
(603) 555-0121
1 (765) 555-0171

7e

✔ **Double-check** your NaturallySpeaking reference card if you forget how to say phone numbers.

F Say Currency

1. Say U.S. dollar amounts normally. For example, say **seven dollars and twenty-five cents** for the first dollar amount. Try these:

$7.25
$5.75
$125.99
$999.95
$1,000,000.54

Double-check your NaturallySpeaking reference card if you forget how to say U.S. currency.

7f

G Say Times of Day

1. Try these times of day. For example, say **ten o'clock PM** and **ten thirty PM** for the first two examples:

10:00 PM	3:26 AM
10:30 PM	1:15 AM
2:00 AM	7:07 PM

2. Try these times. For example, say **ten o'clock** and **twelve o'clock** for the first two examples:

10:00	3:00
12:00	1:00
2:00	

Double-check your NaturallySpeaking reference card if you forget how to say times of day.

7g

H Say Math Formulas

1. Try the following math formulas, combining your symbol creation skills with your numeral skills. For example, in the first formula say **two** *Plus Sign* **two** *Equals Sign* **four** or *Numeral* **two** *Plus Sign Numeral* **two** *Equals Sign Numeral* **four**:

$2 + 2 = 4$	$100 / 50 = 2$
$24 - 12 = 12$	$300 > 100$
$7 * 7 = 49$	$2000 < 4001$

Double-check your NaturallySpeaking reference card if you forget how to say math formulas.

7h

I Say Roman Numerals

1. Try saying the following Roman numerals by saying **Roman** before saying the number, as in **Roman** 3 for *III*:

Roman 1
Roman 2
Roman 3
Roman 4
Roman 5
Roman 6
Roman 7
Roman 8
Roman 9
Roman 10
Roman 25
Roman 50
Roman 100
Roman 2000

7i

Double-check your NaturallySpeaking reference card if you forget how to create Roman numerals.

J Create Numbered Lists

To create a numbered list, say **Numeral <number> Period Space Bar Space Bar** for each item in the list. (You can also say **Press Space Bar**.) Say the first item in the list, then repeat the process, replacing **1** with **2**, then **3**, and so on.

1. Try this numbered list of the presidents of the USA:

Numeral 1 *period* <pause> *Press Space Bar* <pause> *Press Space Bar* <pause> George Washington

Numeral 2 *period* <pause> *Press Space Bar* <pause> *Press Space Bar* <pause> John Adams

Numeral 3 *period* <pause> *Press Space Bar* <pause> *Press Space Bar* <pause> Thomas Jefferson

7j

Double-check your NaturallySpeaking reference card if you need to review how to create numbered lists.

K Format Numbers as Text or Numerals

Sometimes writers are confused about how to handle numbers in text. NaturallySpeaking can also get confused, so Dragon has provided a way to sort things out. To change a number to spelled-out form, select it and say *Format That Spelled Out*. To turn a spelled-out number back into numeral form, select it and say *Format That Number*.

1. Try these examples! Say:

104 <pause> *Select 104* <pause> *Format That Spelled Out*

<pause> *Select one hundred four* <pause> *Format That Number*

2. Try this sentence.

All <pause> *Numeral 5 passengers survived the crash.*

Select Numeral 5 <pause> *Format That Spelled Out*

7k

Double-check your NaturallySpeaking reference card if you forget the two ways to format numbers.

Speaking About...

Numbers in Sentences

Speaking Solutions in This Lesson . . .

A. Use Words for Numbers One Through Ten

B. Use Words for Numbers that Begin a Sentence

C. Use Figures with Weights and Units of Measure

D. Use Figures in Dates and in Addresses

E. Use Figures with Units of Money

F. Use Figures with Temperatures, Room Numbers, and Chapter Numbers

G. Use Figures with the Word *Percent*

Sometimes writers are confused on how to handle numbers in text. Voice Xpress can also get confused, and you will need to spell the numbers out in Spelling Mode.

Consider the following rules about when to spell out numbers.

A. Use Words for Numbers One Through Ten

1. As a general rule, use words for numbers one through ten. For numbers above ten, you can use digits. Try these sentences:

All ten boys arrived on time.

All 29 girls passed the test.

2. Correct and train your errors and repeat the sentences.

F Y I Exceptions to this rule do arise. When writing a technical paper or a specifications document, you can use figures for all numbers.

B. Use Words for Numbers that Begin a Sentence

1. When a number begins a sentence, spell the number out. Try this:

One hundred kids marched down the street.

Forty-seven members attended the meeting.

2. Correct and train your mistakes and repeat the sentences.

C. Use Figures with Weights and Units of Measure

1. With weights and units of measure, use figures. (Often, *pounds* will be abbreviated to *lbs*. This is acceptable in a sentence.) Try these sentences:

He ordered 200 square yards of carpeting.

The carton weighs 7 pounds.

2. Correct and train your errors and repeat both lines.

D. Use Figures in Dates and Addresses

1. Figures are generally used in dates and addresses, but exceptions do exist, as shown below. Try these:

November 25, 2007

1683 North Washington Avenue

One Maple Street

2. Correct and train any errors and repeat the sentences.

E. Use Figures with Units of Money

1. When inserting money values in a sentence, use numbers. Try these:

He owed me $45.50 plus interest.

The entrance fee is $20.

2. Correct and train your errors and repeat the lines.

F. Use Figures with Temperatures, Room Numbers, and Chapter Numbers

1. With temperatures, room numbers, and chapter numbers, use figures. Say this sentence:

It was 78 degrees in Room 12 while I was reading Chapter 12.

2. Correct and train your mistakes and repeat this sentence.

G. Use Figures with the Word Percent

1. Most writing uses figures with the word *percent*. Use figures and the percent symbol (%) only for tables or technical documents. Try this sentence:

He earned a 98 percent on his test.

2. Correct and train your errors and repeat the sentence.

3. Save your work as **Numbers** with the *Save* command.

Think Before You Speak . . .

Read the sentences below and determine which form of each number should be used. Then, at the bottom of your **Numbers** file, create a numbered list and say the sentences, choosing the correct answers from within the parentheses. You may need to train some words, names, and phrases as you go along.

1. (36 *or* Thirty-six) **girls were in the marching band.**

2. (45 *or* Forty-five) **hens laid eggs.**

3. We took (2 *or* two) **men and** (5 *or* five) **women to the conference.**

4. The interest rate on a home mortgage loan is (5.75 *or* five point seventy-five) **this week.**

5. I live at (12 *or* twelve) **Ross Lane.**

6. Give me ($20 *or* twenty dollars) **for dinner.**

7. Please turn to Chapter (2 *or* Two).

8. The temperature in the room was (85 *or* eighty-five) **degrees.**

9. Our approval rating was (75 *or* seventy-five) **percent overall.**

10. (104 *or* One hundred four) **people attended the performance.**

Double-check your answers on the Web at **www.speakingabout.com**. Click the **Speaking About . . . NaturallySeaking** link and select **Speaking About . . . Answers.**

Lesson 8

Navigating Documents

OBJECTIVES In this lesson you will . . .

(A) Dictate Multiple Paragraphs

(B) Move Character by Character

(C) Move Word by Word

(D) Move Line by Line

(E) Move Paragraph by Paragraph and to Beginning and End

In this lesson you will dictate multiple paragraphs and use your document to learn how to move character by character, word by word, line by line, paragraph by paragraph, and from the beginning to the end of the document.

A Dictate Multiple Paragraphs

Before you can move about a document, you must first dictate a full page of text! And it won't take very long, either. The text you are about to dictate will be used in most of the lessons that follow, so correct all the errors and save it in a safe place for later retrieval.

(**NOTE:** This excerpt has been taken from the *Corporate View* series by Barksdale and Rutter, © 2000 by South-Western Educational Publishing. The entire text can be found at **www.corpview.com/Mission-CriticalFunctions/MarketingSales/white2.html**.)

F Y I   Depending on which version of NaturallySpeaking you have installed on your computer, you can use Microsoft Word, WordPerfect, or DragonPad to complete these activities. Choose the writing tool that works best for you!

1. Say the seven-paragraph document on the next page. We have purposely scrambled the paragraphs for a later lesson (Lesson 9, Part D: *Copy, Cut, and Paste Blocks of Text*), so include all the numbers exactly as they appear. Train and correct any new words or mistakes. You will need to train such names and words as *Sherman Poppin*, *Snowboard*, *Snufer*, *Airwalk*, and *K2*.

2. Proofread your document, make corrections, and carefully save this report as **Snowboard** before you continue. You will need the file later.

THE OUTDOOR MARKET

4. It started simple: a hill by the side of a road and a few old board-skis with straps. In the last few years, snowboarding has become a major sport. In fact, it's now an Olympic event. It currently ranks third or fourth in winter sport popularity. By the year 2005, it will likely be the most popular winter sport.

1. We're a society that takes sports—especially outdoor sports—very seriously. According to The New York Times, we take it seriously enough to spend billions each year having fun, most of it out in Mother Nature. Two of the fastest-growing outdoor sports are snowboarding and fly-fishing.

6. Trend watchers have made money by being on top of this new market. By the way, Japan is a new boarding market; in fact, it's one of the fastest-growing new markets. Is it any surprise, then, that many major boarding companies are looking east with a great deal of interest?

7. Where to find a snowboard. The major snowboards are advertised in magazines such as The Snowboarding Zone, Ski and Board, and Western Snowboarding. The major manufacturers of snowboarding equipment are:

Burton

Airwalk

K2

3. How it got started. When Sherman Poppin strapped a couple of skis together and created the first snowboard back in 1965 for his children, few knew it would take off like gangbusters. Poppin called his invention a "Snufer."

2. History of Snowboarding

5. Industry viewpoint. An entire industry has grown up around snowboarding. Careful trend watchers are capitalizing on boarding's popularity. They were in on the ground floor—and now, of course, they are smiling. Snowboarding has increased 148 percent in just a few years. In 1996, 2.4 million people boarded.

Ⓑ Move Character by Character

In this exercise, you will move character by character through Paragraph 4 in your **Snowboard** file. The commands for moving character by character are as follows:

- *Move Right/Forward 1-20 Character(s)*
- *Move Left/Back 1-20 Character(s)*

 When moving one character at a time, you can say *Move Right/Left a Character*, or *Move Right/Left 1 Character*. The word *Characters* is often optional when you use the *Right* and *Left* commands in some programs like Microsoft Word.

1. Position your insertion point on the number *4* near the very top of your **Snowboard** document with your mouse. In the next set of commands you will move several characters to the right and back again. Remember that words in parentheses are optional. Use *Scratch That* to remove errors.

Try this:

Move Right 1 Character
Move Right a Character

Move Left 1 Character
Move Left a Character

Move Right 10 Characters
Move Left 10 Characters

Move Right 1 Character
Move Right 20 Characters
Move Left 1 Character
Move Left 5 Characters

Move Forward 5 Characters
Move Forward 20 Characters
Move Back 20 Characters
Move Back 5 Characters

 Say these movement commands as single phrases. Don't pause between words in the commands. Say *Move Right 10 Characters*, not *Move Right* <pause> *10 Characters*.

2. Position your insertion point on the number *4* again near the very top of your **Snowboard** document. Move forward character by character until you come into contact with each word in this paragraph that has a letter *h* in it. Move right until you land on *hill*, *the*, *with*, *the*, *has*, *third*, *fourth*, *the*, and *the*.

3. Move left again using character commands until you have returned to the word *Olympic*.

8b

✓ **Double-check** your NaturallySpeaking reference card if you forget how to move character by character.

ⓒ Move Word by Word

In this exercise, you will move word by word through Paragraph 4 in your **Snowboard** document. The commands for moving word by word are as follows:

- *Move Right/Forward 1-20 Word(s)*
- *Move Left/Back 1-20 Word(s)*

F Y I When moving one word at a time, you can say either *Move Right/Left a Word* or *Move Right/Left 1 Word*.

1. Position your insertion point on the number *4* near the very top of your **Snowboard** document with your mouse. In the next set of commands you will move several words to the right and back again.

Try this:

Move Right 1 Word
Move Right 5 Words
Move Right 3 Words
Move Right a Word
Move Forward 1 Word
Move Forward 4 Words

Move Left 1 Word
Move Left 5 Words
Move Left 3 Words
Move Back 1 Word
Move Back 4 Words

Move Right 1 Word
Move Right 5 Words
Move Forward 5 Words
Move Left 1 Word
Move Left 2 Words
Move Back 5 Words

2. Position your insertion point on the number *4* again near the very top of your **Snowboard** document. Use your word movement commands and move forward word by word until you come into contact with the first word in each sentence. Move right until you land on *It, In, In, It,* and *By*.

3. Move left again using word movement commands until you have returned to the word *Olympic*.

D Move Line by Line

In this exercise, move line by line through your **Snowboard** file. Here are the commands for moving line by line:

- *Move Up 1-20 (Line(s))*

- *Move Down 1-20 (Line(s))*

- *Move Back 1-20 Line(s)*

- *Move Forward 1-20 Line(s)*

F Y I The word *Lines* is optional with the *Up* and *Down* commands. Say *Lines* if the system seems to hang up. When moving up or down one line at a time, you can say either *Move Up/Down a Line* or *Move Up/Down 1 Line*.

1. Position your insertion point on the number *4* near the very top of your **Snowboard** document with your mouse. In the next set of commands you will move several lines down and back up again.

Try this:

Move Down 1 (Line)
Move Down 5 (Lines)
Move Up 1 (Line)
Move Up 5 (Lines)

Move Down 3 (Lines)
Move Down 7 (Lines)
Move Up 3 (Lines)
Move Up 7 (Lines)

Move Down 10 (Lines)
Move Down 20 (Lines)
Move Up 10 (Lines)
Move Up 20 (Lines)

Move Forward 1 Line
Move Back 1 Line
Move Forward 3 Lines
Move Back 3 Lines

Move Forward 10 Lines
Move Back 10 Lines

2. Position your insertion point on the number *4* near the very top of your **Snowboard** document. Use your line movement commands to move down until you come into contact with the first line in each numbered paragraph.

3. Move up again using the line movement commands until you have returned to Paragraph 6.

8d

Double-check your Voice Xpress reference card if you forget how to move line by line.

Ⓔ Move Paragraph by Paragraph and to Beginning and End

In this exercise, you will move to the beginning and end of lines and paragraphs, and then to the top and bottom of your **Snowboard** document. The commands you will need are as follows:

- *Go to Top*
- *Go to Bottom*
- *Move to/Go to Beginning/Start of Line*
- *Move to/Go to End of Line*
- *Move to/Go to Beginning/Start of Document*
- *Move to/Go to Bottom of Document*

- *Move Up 1-20 Paragraph(s)*
- *Move Down 1-20 Paragraph(s)*
- *Move Back 1-20 Paragraph(s)*
- *Move Forward 1-20 Paragraph(s)*

FYI When moving up or down one paragraph at a time, you can say either *Move Up/Down a Paragraph* or *Move Up/Down 1 Paragraph*. Other options also work, such as *Go/Move to Start/End of Document.*

1. Position your insertion point before the number in Paragraph 6, then try this:

Move to End of Line
Move to Beginning of Line
Move to Beginning of Document
Move to Bottom of Document

Go to Top
Go to Bottom

Go to Beginning of Document
Go to End of Line
Go to Beginning of Line
Go to Bottom of Document

2. Position your insertion point in Paragraph 6, then say this:

Move Up 1 Paragraph
Move Up a Paragraph
Move Down 1 Paragraph
Move Back 1 Paragraph
Move Forward 1 Paragraph

Go to Top

Move Down 4 Paragraphs
Move Up 3 Paragraphs
Move Forward 2 Paragraphs

F Y I Notice that spaces between paragraphs count as paragraphs.

8e

Double-check your NaturallySpeaking reference card if you need to review how to move paragraph by paragraph and to the beginning and end of documents and lines.

Lesson 9

Selecting, Deleting, and Moving Text

OBJECTIVES In this lesson you will . . .

(A) Select and Delete Character by Character

(B) Select and Delete Word by Word

(C) Select and Delete Line by Line, Paragraph by Paragraph, and from Beginning and End

(D) Copy, Cut, and Paste Blocks of Text

In this lesson you will open your **Snowboard** file and learn how to select character by character, word by word, line by line, paragraph by paragraph, and from the beginning and end of the document.

A Select and Delete Character by Character

In this exercise you will use your **Snowboard** file to practice selecting and deleting text character by character. Here are the commands to use for selecting and deleting:

- *Select Next/Previous Character*
- *Select Next/Forward 1-20 Character(s)*
- *Select Previous/Back/Last 1-20 Character(s)*

- *Delete Next/Previous Character*
- *Delete Next/Forward 1-20 Character(s)*
- *Delete Previous/Back/Last 1-20 Character(s)*

F Y I

To clear or unselect any selection, click the document with your mouse or say *Unselect That*. Say *Scratch That* if the commands don't work properly and words appear accidentally. If you have trouble with any of these commands, press the **Ctrl** key as you say them. This will force NaturallySpeaking to recognize what you say only as a command.

1. Open the report you saved as **Snowboard** in Lesson 8. You are going to destroy this file, so make a copy and call it **Destroy This** using the **Save As** command. (**NOTE:** Say *(Click) File, Save As*.) This will preserve a clean copy of your **Snowboard** file for use later in Part D of this lesson.

2. Use your moving skills (Lesson 8) to move your insertion point to the middle of the first sentence in the paragraph beginning with the number *4*:

4. It started simple: a hill by the side of a ro|ad and a few old board-skis with straps.

3. Try selecting and deleting in the following way:

Select Next Character <pause> **Delete That**
Select Previous Character <pause> **Delete That**
Select Next 5 Characters <pause> **Delete That**
Select Previous 5 Characters <pause> **Delete That**
Select Forward 1 Character <pause> **Delete That**
Select Back 1 Character <pause> **Delete That**
Select Forward 5 Characters <pause> **Delete That**
Select Back 5 Characters <pause> **Delete That**
Select Last 2 Characters <pause> **Delete That**

4. Try this method to delete even more quickly:

Delete Next Character
Delete Previous Character
Delete Next 5 Characters
Delete Previous 5 Characters
Delete Forward 3 Characters
Delete Back 3 Characters
Delete Last 4 Characters

5. Expand or contract your selection by trying this:

Select Next Character
Select Forward 2 Characters
Select Next 3 Characters
Select Next 10 Characters
Select Forward 20 Characters
Select Next 20 Characters
Select Back 10 Characters
Select Last 4 Characters
Select Next 10 Characters

Unselect That (This will deselect your selection!)

9a

Double-check your NaturallySpeaking reference card if you forget how to select and delete text character by character.

B Select and Delete Word by Word

Sometimes character selection is impractical and word selection is easier to use. The commands to use for selecting and deleting words are as follows:

- *Select <word> Through <word>* or *Select <word> to <word>*
- *Select Next/Previous Word*
- *Select Next/Forward 1-20 Word(s)*
- *Select Previous/Back/Last 1-20 Word(s)*

- *Delete Next/Previous Word*
- *Delete Next/Forward 1-20 Word(s)*
- *Delete Previous/Back/Last 1-20 Word(s)*

1. Use your **Destroy This** file to learn how to choose multiple words with the *Select <word> Through <word>* or *Select <word> to <word>* commands. Move your insertion point to the middle of the paragraph marked by the number *1*, then say:

   Select **New York** *Through* **Mother Nature**

   <pause> *Delete That*

2. Use your moving skills to position your insertion point once again in the middle of Paragraph 4, then say the following:

   Select Next Word <pause> *Delete That*
   Select Forward 1 Word <pause> *Delete That*
   Select Next 2 Words <pause> *Delete That*
   Select Forward 3 Words <pause> *Delete That*
   Select Last 4 Words <pause> *Delete That*
   Select Previous 3 Words <pause> *Delete That*
   Select Back 2 Words <pause> *Delete That*

   Select Next 20 Words
   Select Forward 20 Words
   Select Previous 10 Words
   Select Back 10 Words

   Unselect That

3. Position your insertion point once again in the middle of Paragraph 5, then say the following quick deletion commands:

   Delete Next Word
   Delete Next 2 Words
   Delete Next 3 Words
   Delete Forward 5 Words

   Delete Previous Word
   Delete Previous 2 Words
   Delete Back 3 Words
   Delete Last 4 Words

4. Using your selection commands, expand and contract your selection of the words in Paragraph 5, then delete each word with the *Delete That* command until the entire paragraph has been erased.

9b

☑️ **Double-check** your NaturallySpeaking reference card if you forget how to select and delete word by word.

Ⓒ Select and Delete Line by Line, Paragraph by Paragraph, and from Beginning and End

Use the following commands to select and delete lines and paragraphs:

- *Select Line*
- *Select Next/Previous Line*
- *Select Next/Forward 1-20 Line(s)*
- *Select Previous/Back/Last 1-20 Line(s)*

- *DeleteLine*
- *Delete Next/Previous Line*
- *Delete Next/Forward 1-20 Line(s)*
- *Delete Previous/Back/Last 1-20 Line(s)*

- *Select Paragraph*
- *Select Next/Previous Paragraph*
- *Select Next/Forward 1-20 Paragraph(s)*
- *Select Previous/Back/Last 1-20 Paragraph(s)*

- *Delete Paragraph*
- *Delete Next/Previous Paragraph*
- *Delete Next/Forward 1-20 Paragraph(s)*
- *Delete Previous/Back/Last 1-20 Paragraph(s)*

1. To practice selecting text and extending and retracting your line and paragraph selections, position your insertion point on Paragraph 4 of your **Destroy This** file and try this:

   Go to Top
   Select Line \<pause\> *Delete That*

   Select Next Paragraph
   Select Next 2 Paragraphs
   Select Forward 3 Paragraphs
   Select Last 2 Paragraphs
   Select Previous Paragraph

   Go to Bottom
   Select Document
   Move Left 1 Character

2. Use CHARACTER selection ONLY to select and delete all the characters in Paragraph 1.

3. Use WORD selection ONLY to select and delete all the words in Paragraph 7.

4. Move to the beginning of the first line in Paragraph 5. Using the *Select Line* and *Delete Line* commands, select and delete each line in the paragraph one by one.

5. Move to Paragraph 6 and use the *Select Paragraph* and *Delete Paragraph* commands to select and delete the paragraph.

6. Move just below Paragraph 3 and delete it with the *Delete Previous Paragraph* command.

7. Use the *Select Document* or *Select All* command, then the *Delete That* command, to select and delete all of the remaining text in the **Destroy This** file.

8. Close the file without saving the changes. After all, you have destroyed it!

9c

☑ Double-check your NaturallySpeaking reference card if you forget how to select and delete lines and paragraphs and extend your selections.

D Copy, Cut, and Paste Blocks of Text

Some of the more important commands to learn include the copy, cut, and paste commands. These commands work just like their mouse-clicking equivalents. Here are the voice commands you will need to accomplish this task:

- *Copy That* or *Copy Selection*
- *Cut That* or *Cut Selection*
- *Paste That*

1. Open the report you saved as **Snowboard** again. (If you haven't yet dictated this report, return to page 2-24, dictate the report, and save it as **Snowboard** before continuing.)

2. You are going to reorganize the paragraphs in this file and place them in the proper order. Use your *Cut That* and *Paste That* commands to move Paragraph 1 into the top spot, as follows:

    a. Move the cursor with your voice to number *1* in what will become the first paragraph.

    b. Use the *Select Paragraph* command to select the paragraph.

    c. Say *Cut That*.

    d. Move your insertion point with your voice below the title, *THE OUTDOOR MARKET*.

    e. Use *New Line* to create spaces if necessary.

    f. Say *Paste That*.

3. Now move the rest of the paragraphs so they are in the correct order, 1–7.

4. After all the paragraphs are in the correct order, resave your edited **Snowboard** file as **Perfect Snowboard** with the *Click File, Save As* command. You will need this file later!

5. Now you are going to expand your **Perfect Snowboard** file. Select all of the text in your document and copy it with the *Copy That* command. Move to the end of your document and paste 3 copies of the entire text at the end of your document. You will then have approximately 4 pages of text.

6. Select two pages of the text you have created and delete them with the *Select Paragraph* and *Delete That* commands, leaving only two copies of your **Perfect Snowboard** report. Save this altered file as **Double Snowboard**.

9d

Double-check your NaturallySpeaking reference card if you need to review how to copy, cut, and paste text.

Lesson 10 | *Formatting Documents*

After all the talking is finished, it's time to make your documents look great. This is called formatting. *Formatting* helps make documents easier to read and gives a professional appearance to your work.

(A) Bold Text

Bolding text is one of the easiest and most frequently used ways to display text clearly. The bolding commands are as follows:

- *Bold That*

- *Restore That* or *Format That (Plain/Normal/Regular)*

1. Open **DragonPad**. Clear your screen and dictate the following sentence, and then select and bold the sentence as shown below:

The biology teacher was speaking about pollution.
<pause> *Select Paragraph*
<pause> *Bold That*

2. Clear your screen. Try bolding, then unbolding with the *Restore That* command.

The environment is a favorite topic of presidential candidates.
<pause> *Select Paragraph*
<pause> *Bold That*
<pause> *Restore That*

10a

Double-check your NaturallySpeaking reference card if you need to review the bold and unbold commands.

B Italicize Text

Italicizing (slanting text upward to the right) is essential for emphasizing the titles of newspapers, magazines, and other printed materials. And—let's be honest—italicized text just looks cool! But be careful not to overuse this option because italicized text can be more difficult to read than normal text. Here are the italicizing commands:

- *Italicize That*
- *Restore That* or *Format That (Plain/Normal/Regular)*

1. Clear your screen and try this sentence, practicing your italicizing skills:

According to The New York Times, we spend billions each year on sports activities.

Select **The New York Times**
Italicize That

2. Clear your screen. Italicize and restore this sentence, then italicize a small section of the sentence:

According to The New York Times, thousands of people voted for the first time.

Select Previous Paragraph (or say *Select Paragraph*)
Italicize That

Select Previous Paragraph (or say *Select Paragraph*)
Restore That

Select **The New York Times**
Italicize That

10b

☑ **Double-check** your NaturallySpeaking reference card if you need to review your italics options.

C Underline Text

Underlined text can be confused with hypertext links and should be avoided. However, there are still places in reports and other printed documents where underlining is acceptable and sets off the text nicely. The underlining commands are as follows:

- *Underline That*
- *Restore That* or *Format That (Plain/Normal/Regular)*

1. Clear your screen and try this sentence, practicing your underlining skills:

There is nothing you can do about it!

Select **nothing**
Underline That

2. Clear your screen and try bolding, italicizing, underlining, and restoring elements of this sentence:

According to U.S. News and World Report, the philanthropist gave $1 million to Mississippi for reading education instruction.

Select Previous Paragraph (or say *Select Paragraph*)
Bold That

Select **U.S. News and World Report**
Italicize That

Select **Mississippi**
Underline That

Select Paragraph
Restore That

3. Take a look at the sentence. What impact did the ***Restore That*** command have on it?

10c

Double-check your NaturallySpeaking reference card if you forget the underlining commands.

D Add Bulleted Lists

Bulleted lists are fun and easy to create in NaturallySpeaking, and they can make a document easier to read by highlighting important points. In this section you will learn the DragonPad and Microsoft Word bullet commands.

1. Clear your screen and try to create a few bullets. NaturallySpeaking may abbreviate the state names. For instance, both *Alaska* and *AK* are acceptable.

These states begin with *A*:

Alabama
Alaska
Arizona
Arkansas

Select Previous 4 Paragraphs

In DragonPad: Say *(Click) Format* <pause> *Bullet Style*

or

In Microsoft Word: Click the **Bullets** button or say *(Click) Format* <pause> *Bullets and Numbering*. Choose the *Bulleted* tab with your voice and choose a bullet style by saying *Move Right/Left* <number> or *Move Up/Down* <number>, then say *(Click) OK*.

2. Clear your screen and try bulleting this list before you create it:

These states begin with *M*:

In DragonPad: Say *(Click) Format* <pause> *Bullet Style*

or

In Microsoft Word: Click the **Bullets** button or say *(Click) Format* <pause> *Bullets and Numbering*. Choose the *Bulleted* tab with your voice and choose a bullet style by saying *Move Right/Left* <number> or *Move Up/Down* <number>, then say *(Click) OK*.

Maine
Massachusetts
Michigan
Minnesota
Mississippi
Missouri
Montana

3. To remove bullets from the list, try this:

Select Previous 7 Paragraphs

In DragonPad: Say *(Click) Format* <pause> *Bullet Style*

or

In Microsoft Word: Click the **Bullets** button or say *(Click) Format* <pause> *Bullets and Numbering*. Choose the *Bulleted* tab with your voice and choose *None*, then say *(Click) OK*.

10d

✓ **Double-check** your NaturallySpeaking reference card if you forget the bullet commands.

E Align Text and Change Fonts

The *alignment*, or *justification*, commands move text to the right or left margin or place text in the center of the page. Centering is often used for headings and other times when you wish to set text apart from the rest of the document. The alignment commands are as follows:

- *Center That* or *Format That Centered*
- *Left Align That* or *Format That Left Aligned*
- *Right Align That* or *Format That Right Aligned*

1. Clear your screen. Try centering this title, then use the ***Left/Right Align That*** commands to move the text to the right and left margins of the page.

Benjamin Franklin: Philosopher, Statesman, Inventor

Say ***Select Line*** <pause> ***Center That***
Left Align That
Right Align That
Center That

2. Choose the text again, and try the alternative alignment commands:

Say ***Select Line***
Format That Left Aligned
Format That Right Aligned
Format That Centered

3. Centering after you have spoken a title is a common occurrence. Clear your screen and dictate the following text about Thomas Jefferson. Align the text and tab the first line of the paragraph, as indicated below:

Thomas Jefferson <pause> ***All Caps That*** <pause> ***Center That***

New Paragraph

Thomas Jefferson was a great philosopher, statesman, and inventor. He lived most of his life in Virginia. He was the third president of the United States.

Select Previous Paragraph
Left Align That

Select **Thomas Jefferson was**
Move Left 1 Character
Tab Key (or say ***Press Tab Key***)

4. Use the Thomas Jefferson text from the previous step to practice changing the font size:

Say ***Select All***
Set Size 8
Set Size 12
Set Size 14
Set Size 18
Unselect That

5. Practice changing to a different font:

Say ***Select All***
Set Font Arial
Set Font Courier
Set Font Times New Roman

6. Practice changing the font and its size in one operation:

Say *Select All*
Set Font Arial 8
Set Font Courier 12
Set Font Times New Roman 14

7. Use the *Format That* option to change the font:

Say *Select All*
Format That Font Arial
Format That Font Courier
Format That Font Times New Roman

10e

Double-check your NaturallySpeaking reference card if you need to review the alignment and font commands.

F Use *What Can I Say?*

What if you can't find your reference card and forget a command, or what if you want to learn some new options? Try the *What Can I Say?* command. (**NOTE:** This feature isn't available in some *Standard* and *Essential* versions of NaturallySpeaking. If it isn't available in your version, simply use your mouse to select the **Help** button.)

1. Open NaturallySpeaking.

2. Try opening the **What Can I Say?** help window with this command:

What Can I Say?

3. Scroll down the list of commands and select two that you haven't used before. For example, select **Command List, Formatting Text** (as shown in Figure 2-1) and review the formatting commands. Give them a try!

10f

Double-check your NaturallySpeaking reference card if you forget the *What Can I Say?* command.

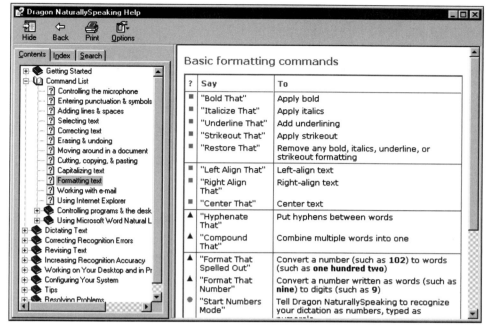

figure 2-1

The *What Can I Say* Window

Basic formatting commands

?	Say	To
■	"Bold That"	Apply bold
■	"Italicize That"	Apply italics
■	"Underline That"	Add underlining
■	"Strikeout That"	Apply strikeout
■	"Restore That"	Remove any bold, italics, underline, or strikeout formatting
■	"Left Align That"	Left-align text
■	"Right Align That"	Right-align text
■	"Center That"	Center text
▲	"Hyphenate That"	Put hyphens between words
▲	"Compound That"	Combine multiple words into one
▲	"Format That Spelled Out"	Convert a number (such as **102**) to words (such as **one hundred two**)
▲	"Format That Number"	Convert a number written as words (such as **nine**) to digits (such as **9**)
●	"Start Numbers Mode"	Tell Dragon NaturallySpeaking to recognize your dictation as numbers, typed as numerals

Speaking About...

Reports

Speaking Solutions in This Lesson . . .

A. Format an unbound report

B. Print your report

A. Format an Unbound Report

The unbound report is a simple, yet formal, report style. Format your **Perfect Snowboard** file as shown on the next page. Start by deleting the numbers. Use your mouse or your keyboard as little as possible as you format the entire document.

Bold, all caps

THE OUTDOOR MARKET

4 spaces

Italicize *The New York Times*

We're a society that takes sports—especially outdoor sports—very seriously. According to *The New York Times,* we take it seriously enough to spend billions each year having fun, most of it out in Mother Nature. Two of the fastest-growing outdoor sports are snowboarding and fly-fishing.

History of Snowboarding ← Initial caps on internal headings

How it got started. When Sherman Poppin strapped a couple of skis together and created the first snowboard back in 1965 for his children, few knew it would take off like gangbusters. Poppin called his invention a "Snufer."

It started simple: a hill by the side of a road and a few old board-skis with straps. In the last few years, snowboarding has become a major sport. In fact, it's now an Olympic event. It currently ranks third or fourth in winter sport popularity. By the year 2005, it will likely be the most popular winter sport.

← Double-space between paragraphs

Industry viewpoint. An entire industry has grown up around snowboarding. Careful trend watchers are capitalizing on boarding's popularity. They were in on the ground floor—and now, of course, they are smiling. Snowboarding has increased 148 percent in just a few years. In 1996, 2.4 million people boarded.

Cap only the first letter of side headings and end with a period

Trend watchers have made money by being on top of this new market. By the way, Japan is a new boarding market; in fact, it's one of the fastest-growing new markets. Is it any surprise, then, that many major boarding companies are looking east with a great deal of interest?

Single-space paragraphs

Where to find a snowboard. The major snowboards are advertised in magazines such as *The Snowboarding Zone, Ski and Board,* and *Western Snowboarding.* The major manufacturers of snowboarding equipment are:

Italicize magazine names

- Burton
- Airwalk ← Bullet the list
- K2

B. Print Your Report

1. Resave your **Perfect Snowboard** file with the name **Most Perfect Snowboard**.

2. Print your report by saying the *(Click) File, Print* command in Windows or by clicking **File→Print**.

G Transfer Text to Microsoft Word or Other Programs

To finalize your document's format, you may need to transfer it to your favorite word processor. There are a few ways to transfer text from NaturallySpeaking to other selected software applications:

- You can save your text in a file format the other application can understand, such as RTF or TXT format. Then you can open the document in most word processing programs.

  - **.rtf Rich Text Format:** A Microsoft format that preserves the formatting of the text; it is compatible with most word processing programs, especially Microsoft Word.

  - **.txt TeXT Format:** A common format that doesn't preserve formatting; this is the most universal format.

  - **.doc Word DOCument format:** A Microsoft format used for Microsoft Word.

  - **wpd WordPerfect Document format:** A Corel WordPerfect format used for WordPerfect.

- Use the normal ***Copy That*** and ***Paste That*** commands. To copy large amounts of text, you can say ***Copy All to Clipboard***. This will save a copy on the Windows clipboard for pasting into another software application or document.

1. Open a copy of your **Perfect Snowboard** file.

2. Open the application you want the text copied to, such as Microsoft Word or Corel WordPerfect.

3. Transfer text from the NaturallySpeaking DragonPad dictation window to your target word processing application. For example, if your target application is Microsoft Word, use the ***Copy All to Clipboard, Switch to Microsoft Word,*** and ***Paste That*** commands, in this order.

10g

Double-check your NaturallySpeaking reference card if you forget how to transfer text.

section 3

Speaking Solutions for Your Career

You've learned the basics of speech recognition. Nevertheless, you're probably feeling a bit awkward using your voice as a writing tool. It's a natural feeling. It takes practice to remember all the tips and tricks of your voice software. As in driving a car for the first time, you will need to practice before the procedures become automatic. As with most things, practice makes the difference.

To help you make your voice skills an automatic part of your computer routine, we're giving you a few honest-to-goodness, career-related scenarios to practice. Elements of these scenarios have been written to support speech recognition instruction in other courses by Delmar and South-Western Educational Publishing.

In the sections that follow, you'll experience how speech recognition can be used in typical marketing, medical, legal, human resources, and corporate communications situations. To start you off, we have included a few resume and job application exercises so you can see how speech recognition can help you advance your own career.

To make your work as realistic as possible, we are going to use a business story line or scenario. In this scenario, you will be applying for the position of marketing assistant for a fictitious major medical supply and pharmaceutical manufacturing company called MediView. This position will allow you to see how speech recognition is being used in a variety of medical and dental careers. As an added bonus, you will experience firsthand how marketing, public relations, human resources, and corporate communications office professionals are benefiting from these breakthrough voice technologies. You will even need to meet with the legal department on several issues, which will give you a chance to learn how speech is used in that field, too.

So jump into the scenario, practice your speech skills, and "speak" your way into a new career!

Activity 1 | *A Job Description for MediView*

OBJECTIVES   In this activity you will...

(A) Dictate a job description for a medical marketing position

(B) Dictate medical careers

(C) Prepare a job description of your own

(D) Dictate medical definitions and terminology

Speaking About... Proofreaders' Marks

Speech recognition has found a home in business offices of all kinds, particularly in the medical and legal professions. In the pages that follow, you will apply your skills to some of these true-to-life tasks.

The good place to start a job search is looking at job descriptions. Job descriptions detail the work employees are asked to perform. In this scenario, you're looking to apply for a marketing position at MediView. This experience will help you learn the speech recognition skills you need to help you obtain a job in your chosen career.

Say This!

1. Examine and dictate the job description for a marketing position shown on the next page. You may need to train several words, such as *ambulatory* and *paramedic*. Use your Correction window to train acronyms such as *HMO*.

2. Save this job description as **Sample Job Description.**

TITLE: MARKETING ASSISTANT – MEDICAL SPECIALTY

Date Posted: January 1, 2002
Date Closed: January 15, 2002
Department or Group: MediView Marketing Team

Working Environment: At MediView, a division of Corporate View, our highest priority is our people: our employees and our customers. We pride ourselves on a workforce that possesses problem solving, time management, and interpersonal skills. Our employees are self-motivated, which helps us maintain the highest possible productivity. We invite you to consider working in this exciting, team-oriented environment.

Location: Boulder, Colorado

Main Responsibilities: Facilitate communications and public relations between the MediView marketing team and our customers. A typical MediView customer would be a medical professional working in a hospital, ambulatory care facility, or for a health maintenance organization (HMO) in one of the following positions:

- Medical office managers and assistants

- Registered and licensed practical nurses, including hospital nurses and office nurses

- Physicians

- Physician assistants

- Emergency medical technicians and paramedics

- Occupational and physical therapists

- Respiratory therapists

- Speech-language pathologists

- Clinical laboratory technicians

Education, Skills, and Experience: Requires an associate's or bachelor's degree in English, corporate communications, journalism, public relations, or business writing. Marketing experience preferred. Background in medical terminology highly recommended.

Salary Range: Competitive salary range is $34,000–$45,000.

Dictate the Definitions

In the job description you just dictated, MediView is asking for a "background in medical terminology." If you are going to market to and communicate with medical professionals, you had better learn their language!

The specialized terminology professionals use on the job is called "shoptalk." Knowing the shoptalk for the industry in which you are working is vital. Before your interview with MediView, you may wish to prepare by reading a book like *Comprehensive Medical Assisting: Administrative and Clinical Competencies* by Wilburta Lindh et al., or *Terminology for Allied Health Professionals* by Carolee Sormunen. This background will help you learn many of the medical terms used daily in the medical supply industry.

Dictate the medical-related terms and definitions shown on the next page. (**NOTE:** Asterisks which appear after some of the definitions indicate the source reference at the bottom of the page. Do not dictate the asterisks.) Save this file as **Definitions**.

Ambulatory care setting – health care environment where services are provided on an outpatient basis. The word *ambulatory* is from Latin and means "capable of walking." Examples include the solo-physician's office, the group practice, the urgent care center, and the health maintenance organization.*

Ambulatory care facility – a medical facility or setting that offers ambulatory care.

Pharmacology – study of drugs; the science concerned with the history, origin, sources, physical and chemical properties, and uses of drugs and their effects on living organisms.*

Health maintenance organization (HMO) – type of managed care operation that is typically set up as a for-profit corporation with salaried employees. There are two types: HMOs "with walls" offer a range of medical services under one roof; HMOs "without walls" typically contract with physicians in the community to provide patient services for an agreed-upon fee.*

Medical office management – work that involves such tasks as office organization, communications, reception, charting, billing, payroll, and scheduling in medical offices and other ambulatory care facilities like hospitals and HMOs.

*From Wilburta Lindh et al., *Comprehensive Medical Assisting: Administrative and Clinical Competencies.* (Albany, NY: Delmar/Thomson Learning, 1998), G-2, G-4, and G-11.

Dictate These Professions

Knowing about the jobs people perform can help you be a more successful marketer of products to your target customers. This section focuses on health care professionals that order and use MediView products. As you can see, there are various specialties in the medical profession. Each of these descriptions is based on information in the *Occupational Outlook Handbook* published by the Bureau of Labor Statistics. It can be found online at **http://stats.bls.gov**.

Dictate three of the seven professions displayed on the next page. Create a **Professions** file and save these medical specialties in your document. Train any words that may come up incorrectly, like *therapist* and *cerebral*.

Physician (MD) – will diagnose illnesses and prescribe and administer treatment for people suffering from injury or disease. A physician will examine patients, obtain medical histories, and order, perform, and interpret medical tests. A physician may become a general practitioner of family medicine or may choose a specialty such as surgery, plastic surgery, cardiology, or radiology. A physician may work long, irregular hours.

There were more than 577,000 physicians in 1998. Seven out of ten were office-based in clinics and HMOs. Approximately two out of every ten physicians were employed by hospitals.

To become a physician requires a tremendous amount of education. Most start with four years of undergraduate school, then go on to four years of medical school and 3-8 years of internship or residency, depending on the specialty the physician has selected. The salary range for a physician extends from $120,000.00–$250,000.00 annually.

Physician Assistant (PA) – will provide health care services under the supervision of a physician. A physician assistant should not be confused with the medical assistant, who performs routine clerical tasks. A physician assistant works as a member of the health care team, taking medical histories, examining patients, and ordering laboratory tests and X rays.

A physician assistant will generally work 40 hours per week, although the hours may be irregular. About 67 percent of jobs were in offices and clinics working with physicians, dentists, or other health practitioners. About 21 percent work in hospitals.

To become a physician assistant usually requires at least two years of college and two years of additional training. The salary range is $25,000.00–$71,000.00.

Emergency Medical Technician (EMT) – will be dispatched to the scene of an accident or emergency. Will assist victims of automobile accidents, heart attacks, drownings, emergency childbirth, and gunshot wounds that require immediate medical attention. An EMT or paramedic will also see to the safe transportation of injured patients.

There were approximately 115,000 EMTs in 1998. Additionally, there are many who volunteer in smaller cities, towns, and rural areas. An EMT will earn over $20,000.00 a year. An EMT might be employed by a hospital or a fire department.

Training is offered on many levels starting with EMT-basic or EMT-1, then progressing to EMT-2, EMT-3, and EMT-paramedic or EMT-4. At each level the EMT receives more in-depth training and is certified to assist with a greater variety of life-threatening medical conditions.

Occupational or Physical Therapist – will work with individuals who have conditions that are mentally, physically, or emotionally disabling. An occupational therapist will help people improve their ability to perform tasks in their daily living and working environments. A physical therapist provides services that help restore function, improve mobility, relieve pain, and prevent or limit physical disabilities. They restore, maintain, and promote overall fitness and health, for example, assisting in the recovery from carpal tunnel syndrome (CTS), a knee injury, or a leg injury.

Occupational and physical therapists normally work 40-hour weeks, which may include some evenings and weekends. There were 120,000 jobs in physical therapy in 1998. There were about 73,000 occupational therapists working in 1998. One in four works part time.

Physical and occupational therapists must receive a license by passing an exam. Most receive bachelor's degrees and many receive master's degrees. The salary range is $38,000.00–$65,000.00.

Respiratory Therapist – will evaluate, treat, and care for patients with breathing disorders. A respiratory therapist will test the lung capacity of patients and analyze oxygen and carbon dioxide concentrations. A respiratory therapist will generally work between 35-40 hours a week. They may work evenings, nights, or weekends.

A respiratory therapist must receive specialized post-high school training to become a registered respiratory therapist (RRT) or complete a shorter program of study to become a certified respiratory therapist (CRT). These programs may take 1-2 years to complete. Salaries range between $25,000.00-$47,000.00 a year.

Speech-Language Pathologist – will assess, treat, and help prevent speech, language, communication, voice, swallowing, fluency, and other related disorders. A speech-language pathologist will work with people who cannot make speech sounds, or cannot make them clearly. This includes conditions like stuttering or the inability to speak caused by stroke, cerebral palsy, hearing loss, or brain injury. Speech recognition technology is often used to help individual patients speak clearly.

There were about 105,000 jobs in 1998. Many work in schools. To practice this profession requires a state license. Most states require a master's degree level of study. Salaries ranged between $34,000.00-$80,000.00 each year.

Clinical Laboratory Technician – will work in a laboratory to detect, diagnose, and treat disease. A laboratory technician will examine and analyze body fluids, tissues, and cells looking for bacteria, parasites, and other microorganisms. They will also analyze the chemical content of fluids, match blood for transfusions, and test for drug levels in a patient's blood. Most will earn $25,000.00–$48,000.00 for a year. Laboratory technicians keep regular hours. Usually a bachelor's or master's degree is required. School subjects include chemistry, biological sciences, microbiology, mathematics, and other specialized courses.

Speak for Yourself!

Prepare another job description for a medical career that interests you. Use the information provided in the *Dictate These Professions* section to help you compose your job description. Include each element found in your **Sample Job Description** as described here:

Title: Dictate the profession you have selected
Date Posted: Today's date
Date Closed: Two weeks from today's date
Department or Group: Describe the team this person would be a part of, such as *Laboratory Research Team*, *Hospital Emergency Team*, or *HMO Medical Team*
Location: List a city and state where you would like to live and work
Working Environment: Describe a hospital, laboratory, HMO, or doctor's clinic setting
Main Responsibilities: Compose your answer based on the information provided in the *Dictate These Professions* section
Education, Skills, and Experience: Pull your information from the *Dictate These Professions* section
Salary Range: List the salary range found in the *Dictate These Professions* section

Save your document as **My Job Description**.

Proofreaders' Marks

Proofreaders' marks are symbols, letters, or words used to mark corrections or changes on printed documents. Use the marks shown on the following page when editing your documents or reviewing documents for others.

Proofreaders' Marks

Capitalize	Cap or ≡
Close up	⌒
Delete	ℓ
Insert	∧
Insert comma	⋏
Insert space	#
Insert apostrophe	⌄
Insert quotation marks	⌄⌄ ⌄⌄
Move right	]
Move left	[
Move down; lower	⌐ ⌐
Move up; raise	⌐ ⌐
Lowercase	lc or /
Paragraph	¶
No new paragraph	no ¶
Align copy	‖
Spell out	sp
Let it stand; ignore correction	stet or ---
Transpose	tr or ⌣
Underline or Italics	___ or ital

Print copies of both your **Sample Job Description** and **My Job Description** documents and proof-read them carefully. Use the proofreaders' symbols to mark your errors. Reopen your speech soft-ware and fix the mistakes. Resave your files.

Activity 2 | *A Cover Letter for MediView*

OBJECTIVES In this activity you will...

Ⓐ Dictate a cover letter for a medical marketing position

Ⓑ Prepare a cover letter of your own

Ⓒ Dictate medical definitions, terminology and career information

Ⓓ Think before you speak

Speaking About... Confusing Terms 1

The first thing you must do if you want to get a job is to apply! This requires a cover letter, which will introduce you and your resume to a prospective employer. The position you will be applying for is at MediView, a division of Corporate View. Let's suppose that Corporate View is a large multinational manufacturing corporation that began developing emergency first response, rescue, and first aid equipment about two decades ago. The MediView division has been very successful and has expanded into manufacturing medical tools and devices of all kinds. MediView's mission is to find solutions for illnesses and injuries that affect people's ability to live healthy, active lives.

"A letter of introduction may be the most important correspondence you ever write" (Barksdale and Rutter, *Online Resume and Job Search* [Cincinnati: South-Western Educational Publishing, 2000], 92). This letter introduces you to the Human Resources personnel at MediView who can change your career and provide you with an employment opportunity of a lifetime. There are four goals you must accomplish in a cover letter. You must:

1. State specifically what job you are applying for.
2. Introduce your strongest and most relevant qualifications for the job.
3. Invite the prospective employer to review your qualifications in more detail in your accompanying resume.
4. Ask for an interview.

Before you try writing a couple of cover letters, review the following *Speaking About* section for some confusing words you may need to know to complete the *Say This!* section.

Confusing Terms 1

Speaking Solutions in This Activity...

A. Choose properly between the words *all ready* and *already*

B. Choose properly between the words *advise* and *advice*

C. Choose properly between the words *assistants* and *assistance*

D. Choose properly between the words *aides*, *aids*, and *AIDS*

As you dictate the sample letter in the next *Say This!* section, you may have difficulty with words like *all ready* and *already*. Even before speech recognition existed, many writers confused the meaning of these and other tricky words. The problem is compounded with speech recognition because the terms sound very similar to each other. It is very easy to say *already* (without a pause) when you mean to say *all* <pause> *ready*. *Advice* and *advise* are very similar in sound but different in meaning, as are *aids*, *aides*, and *AIDS*. *Assistance* and *assistants* also sound similar, so you must speak them clearly and proofread to make sure they have been used correctly.

 Your speech software is great at guessing alternative word choices. With most similar words, if you select or **Correct** the word to replace it, the next logical alternative normally appears! For example, if you select *advice*, chances are *advise* will appear automatically as the next best alternative in the Correction window.

Read the following definitions and say the examples. Be certain you understand the differences. Then, answer the questions that follow in the *Think Before You Speak!* section.

A. Choose Properly Between the Words *All Ready* and *Already*

- *All ready* means *completely or wholly ready* or *prepared*. Try dictating these examples:

    As soon as you are all ready, we'll leave for the show.
    I'll begin the exam when you are all ready.

- *Already* is an adverb that means *previously* or *by a specified or implied time*. Try saying these samples:

    I've already seen that movie three times.
    By the time I arrived, she had already left for school.

B. Choose Properly Between the Words *Advise* and *Advice*

- *Advise* is a verb that means *to offer counsel or suggestions*. Try these two sentences:

    I advise you not to attend that concert.
    Parents often advise their children.

- *Advice* is a noun that means *specific recommendations* or *suggestions*. Try these:

    My advice to you is simple: Don't worry.
    A mother's advice is often the best advice.

C. Choose Properly Between the Words *Assistants* and *Assistance*

- *Assistants* are *people who aid, help, or assist.* Try these examples:

   The assistants began to help the injured.
   The class was taught by seven assistants.

- *Assistance* is a noun that means *help* or *aid.* Try this:

   They gave assistance to the injured.
   The volunteers gave assistance to the class.

D. Choose Properly Between the Words *Aides*, *Aids*, and *AIDS*

- *Aides* are *people who act as assistants.* Try this example:

   The aides began to help the injured.

- *Aids* is the plural form of the noun *aid* that means *something, like a device, that gives assistance.* Try this:

   They gave hearing aids to the patients at the nursing home.
   The instructional aids helped students understand the medical risks.

- *AIDS* is the acronym for a disease caused by the HIV virus. Try this:

   They treated him for AIDS in the hospital.

Save your work as **Confusing 1**.

Think Before You Speak...

Choose the correct form of the word in parentheses and then dictate each of the following sentences. Add them to your **Confusing 1** file.

I've (already *or* all ready) **seen that movie.**

We'll leave as soon as you are (already *or* all ready)**.**

What (advise *or* advice) **do you have for me?**

How would you (advise *or* advice) **me in this situation?**

My mom (already *or* all ready) **gave me permission.**

My (advise *or* advice) **to you is practice makes perfect.**

The (assistants *or* assistance) **provided** (assistants *or* assistance) **to the patients.**

The (aides, aids, *or* AIDS) **assisted the** (aides, aids, *or* AIDS) **victims that were confined to the hospital.**

The (aides, aids, *or* AIDS) **displayed a variety of visual** (aides, aids, *or* AIDS) **to teach CPR to the paramedics.**

Double-check your answers on the Web at **www.speakingabout.com**. As the site opens, select the link for your specific speech program and click the **Speaking About . . . Answers** link.

Say This!

1. Open your speech recognition software and dictate the cover letter shown below. Be sure to include all the parts that are indicated, but don't dictate the descriptive copy that appears shaded. Use the ***Paragraph*** and ***Line*** commands to adjust the spacing between each part of the letter. You may need to train a few phrases like *Up-Start Tech*.

April 12, 2002 ◄——— Date

4 spaces

Attention: Mr. Mark Mitchell ◄——————— Inside Address
Human Resources Department
MediView
One Corporate View Drive
Boulder, Colorado 80303-0103

Double-space

Dear Mr. Mitchell ◄——— Salutation

Double-space   Single-space each paragraph

Our university job placement center already posted a notice advertising a marketing assistant position in the MediView division. Please advise me whether I am still eligible to interview for this position.

Double-space

My training is in corporate communications and public relations, but I am intensely interested in the medical field. As a marketing assistant at MediView, I can help improve communications with your medical customers and clients.

Double-space

I have excellent communication and writing skills. I am willing to take any advice that will improve my job performance. While working my way through college, I demonstrated leadership by managing the public relations activities for Up-Start Tech. In each of my performance reviews, I received the highest possible score for job quality and teamwork.

Double-space

Please see my enclosed resume for details about the many ways I can benefit your company. I am prepared to relocate to Boulder should the job be offered to me. I would welcome an interview with you at your convenience. You can reach me by phone at (791) 555-0134 most evenings or contact me by email at mills@speakingabout.com.

Double-space

Thank you for your consideration.

Cordially yours ◄——— Complimentary close

4 spaces   ◄——— Signature

Robin Mills

2. Save your letter as **Sample Cover Letter**.

Dictate These Professions

Knowing all about the jobs people do in the professions to which you are marketing and selling is vital. This section focuses on nurses. There are various specialties and working situations that registered nurses (RNs) and licensed practical nurses (LPNs) occupy. Each of the descriptions shown on the next page is based on information from the *Occupational Outlook Handbook* published by the Bureau of Labor Statistics. It can be found online at **http://stats.bls.gov**. Open your **Professions** file and add these nursing positions to the bottom of your list. Train words that may come up incorrectly, such as *regimens* and *Alzheimer's*.

Registered Nurse (RN) – will work to promote health, prevent disease, and help patients cope with illness. A registered nurse is an advocate and health educator for patients, families, and communities. When providing direct patient care, an RN will observe, assess, record symptoms, reactions, and progress; assist physicians during treatments and examinations; administer medications; and assist in convalescence and rehabilitation.

There were over 2.1 million registered nurses in 1998. About three out of five work in hospitals. Others work in offices and clinics. The average salary range is $29,000.00–$69,000.00 annually. Registered nurses often work irregular hours.

Licensed Practical Nurse (LPN) – will help care for sick, injured, or disabled patients under the direction of physicians and registered nurses. A licensed practical nurse, called licensed vocational nurse in Texas and California, will check for vital signs like blood pressure, pulse, and breathing; collect samples from patients for testing; and see to the personal needs of patients.

Licensed practical nurses held about 692,000 jobs in 1998. Of this total, 32 percent worked in hospitals, 28 percent worked in nursing homes, and 14 percent worked in clinics or HMOs. The salary range is $26,000.00–$37,500.00 a year.

Nurses, both RNs and LPNs, work in a variety of situations and environments:

Hospital Nurse – is in the largest group of nurses. Most hospital nurses are staff nurses who provide bedside nursing care and carry out medical regimens. The hospital nurse must also supervise licensed practical nurses and aides. The hospital nurse is usually assigned to one area such as surgery, maternity, pediatrics, emergency room, intensive care, or treatment of cancer patients.

Office Nurse – assists physicians in private practice, clinics, outpatient surgery centers, emergency medical centers, and health maintenance organizations (HMOs). An office nurse prepares patients for and assists with examinations, administers injections and medications, dresses wounds and incisions, assists with minor surgery, and maintains records. Routine laboratory and office work is also performed.

Nursing Home Nurse – manages nursing care for residents having conditions ranging from a fracture to Alzheimer's disease; assesses residents' medical conditions; develops treatment plans; supervises other nurses and nursing aides; performs difficult procedures such as starting intravenous fluids; and works in a specialty care department, such as a long-term rehabilitation unit for strokes and head injuries.

Occupational Health or Industry Nurse – provides nursing care at work to employees, customers, and others with minor injuries and illnesses. An occupational health or industry nurse provides emergency care, prepares accident reports, and arranges for future care if necessary. This type of nurse also offers health counseling, assists with health examinations and inoculations, and assesses work environments to identify potential health or safety problems.

Speak for Yourself!

Now that you have dictated a sample cover letter, prepare one of your own. You may apply for either the marketing assistant position at MediView, a nursing position, or another job for which you would like to prepare a cover letter. Keep your cover letter at less than one page in length. Include all the proper spacing and the personal information necessary for a prospective employer to contact you.

As you write, remember these four guidelines:

- State specifically what job you are applying for

- Introduce your strongest and most relevant qualifications for the job

- Invite the prospective employer to review your qualifications in more detail in your accompanying resume

- Ask for an interview

Save your letter as **My Cover Letter**.

Print both your **Sample Cover Letter** and **My Cover Letter** and proofread them. Use your proof-readers' symbols to mark errors. Make corrections and resave your documents.

Activity 3 | *Preparing a Resume for MediView*

OBJECTIVES In this activity you will...

Speaking About... Colons and Semicolons (Online)

(A) Dictate a resume for a medical marketing position

(B) Prepare a resume of your own

You have done a great job preparing your cover letter and you have studied many of the medical terms you may need to use in the interview and on the job. However, you must also submit a resume with your cover letter in order to be considered for the position.

Resumes can be submitted in hard copy form (that is, on paper), or they can be submitted online in a variety of ways. More and more, online submission is becoming the preferred way to submit resumes—especially to large corporations and organizations. However, before you can finalize a good online resume, you should prepare several of them in printed form so you can carefully analyze the words you use. To study how to do this in more detail, review the book *Online Resume and Job Search* by Barksdale and Rutter, © 2000 by South-Western Educational Publishing.

→ Speaking About...

Colons and Semicolons (Online)

Before you begin speaking your resumes, take a few minutes, visit the www.speakingabout.com web site, and review online the rules for semicolon and colon usage. Using semicolons and colons correctly helps your resume and other documents read smoothly and clearly. Mastery of these marks also signals to the reader that your material is carefully composed and well thought out. Properly using these two punctuation marks can make your writing easier to read, which is the goal of every resume!

Go to www.speakingabout.com. As the site opens, select the book you are using and click **Speaking About... Colons and Semicolons**. Follow the online instructions. After you complete the online *Think Before You Speak* exercises, check your answers by choosing the Speaking About . . . Answers link.

Say This!

1. Dictate and examine the resume shown on the next page. You may need to train some of the words: *Walla Walla*, *Pullman*, *Intranet*, and *Up-Start Tech*.

2. After you have finished dictating, save your document as **Sample Resume**.

Linda Miller
2813 Orchard Drive
Walla Walla, Washington 99362-0136
(509) 555-0123
miller@speakingabout.com
www.speakingabout.com

Work Objective

A full-time job in communications or public relations in a medical supply company

Related Experience

- Manage public relations activities for Up-Start Tech
- Write press releases, white papers, summaries, letters, memos, email, web pages, and other interoffice communications for Up-Start Tech
- Volunteered ten hours a week at Walla Walla County Hospital
- As a teenager, I worked summers as an aide to a registered nurse
- Served as an editor for high school and college newspapers
- Learned to research using the corporate Intranet while working at Up-Start Tech
- Proficient with speech recognition software (over 130 words per minute with 98 percent accuracy)
- Efficient with word processing, spreadsheet, database, and presentation software

Education

Washington State University, Pullman, Washington. BS major: Marketing; Minor: Corporate Communications. April 17, 2001, GPA 3.72

Experience

Volunteer: Summers 1999, 2000
Walla Walla County Hospital

Manager of Public Relations: August 15, 2001 to present
Up-Start Tech, Walla Walla, Washington

References

References available upon request

Speak for Yourself!

Use what you have learned when dictating a sample resume to prepare a resume of your own that you can submit for a job you would like to have. Keep your resume at one page in length. Include all the proper spacing and the personal information necessary for a prospective employer to contact you.

Save your document as **My Resume**.

Print both your **Sample Resume** and **My Resume** and proofread them. Use your proofreaders' symbols to mark errors. Make corrections and resave your documents.

Activity 4 | *Preparing for the MediView Interview*

OBJECTIVES   In this activity you will...

(A) Dictate answers to interview questions for a medical marketing position

(B) Dictate medical definitions and terminology

(C) Prepare possible interview questions of your own and answer them

Are you ready to go to work at MediView? Well, you have one more hurdle to pass over before you can take the job. It's the interview!

With your cover letter and resume submitted to the Human Resources (HR) department at MediView, you are in the running for the medical marketing assistant position. The HR team will now screen the applications, cover letters, and resumes and find the top three to five candidates. Those candidates will be called for an interview.

Interviews often make people very nervous. Speech recognition can help you overcome your interviewing fears by helping you prepare verbal answers to interview questions. Because you speak your answers instead of just keying them, you have a chance to practice responding verbally and in writing simultaneously to any questions your interviewers can possibly throw at you. Practice in speaking your answers will help you interview more confidently.

To help candidates prepare, HR departments will sometimes submit sample interview questions to them in advance. Regardless, you should prepare a list of possible interview questions of your own and prepare answers for each of them. Answering these questions with your voice software will help give you confidence.

Say This!

1. Dictate the sample interview questions shown on the following page, and then answer each one. Limit your answers to 25–50 words. Use full sentences. You may need to train some of the words.

2. After you have finished dictating, save your document as **Sample Interview Questions**.

1. This job, of course, requires communicating with medical professionals. What skills do you have that will help you communicate with physicians, nurses, and paramedics?

   _____

   _____

2. Many excellent marketing and communications candidates want to work at MediView, yet they are not familiar with medical terminology. What can you do to learn the medical shoptalk?

   _____

   _____

3. What, in your opinion, are the types of injuries and illnesses treated by RNs in ambulatory settings?

   _____

   _____

4. We sell medical tools, surgical implements, and health care devices to HMOs. There are two kinds of HMO. What are they?

   _____

   _____

5. What is an EMT? Explain EMT training.

   _____

   _____

Dictate the Definitions

Knowing the shoptalk for the industry in which you are working is vital. Open your **Definitions** file and dictate the following definitions at the bottom of your list.

Carpal Tunnel Syndrome (CTS) – "an inflammatory disorder that affects the carpal–or wrist–part of a specific nerve. Repetitive stress, physical trauma, certain diseases, or specific hereditary conditions can inflame the sheaths that surround wrist tendons. With the swelling of small blood vessels, pressure increases on the nerve and disrupts its function. The result is numbness, pain and a loss of manual dexterity. CTS treatment usually consists of rest, splinting the wrist and anti-inflammatory drugs. Severe cases require surgery to relieve the pressure."*

Repetitive Strain Injury (RSI) – caused by repeated physical movements. RSI can damage nerves, tendons, and muscles. Occupations at risk for RSI include: musicians, meatpackers, truck drivers, and office workers using computer keyboards and a mouse. The repetitive motions of these and other occupations can result in injuries of the hands, arms, back, and shoulders.

Biohazard – material that has been in contact with body fluid and is capable of transmitting disease.**

Ergonomics – scientific study of work and space, including factors that influence workers' productivity and affect workers' health.***

*Dr. Thomas W. Orme, "Carpal Tunnel Syndrome: Is Keyboarding Bad for Your Health?" *Drkoop.com Exclusive* (January 2000). Available: http://www.drkoop.com/news/focus/january/cts.html

**From Wilburta Lindh et al., *Comprehensive Medical Assisting: Administrative and Clinical Competencies.* (Albany, NY: Delmar/Thomson Learning, 1998), G-3.

***From Wilburta Lindh et al., *Comprehensive Medical Assisting: Administrative and Clinical Competencies.* (Albany, NY: Delmar/Thomson Learning, 1998), G-9.

Speak for Yourself!

Now that you've dictated sample interview questions, prepare three additional interview questions of your own that may be asked in a typical job interview. Keep your answers to about 50 words each.

Save your letter as **My Interview Questions**.

Print both your **Sample Interview Questions** and **My Interview Questions** and proofread them. Use your proofreaders' symbols to mark errors. Make corrections and resave your documents.

Debriefing

Congratulations; you get the job! You were the most qualified candidate, after all. Now it's time to get down to work. In the sections that follow, you will be given several assignments that will help the MediView division of Corporate View market and sell its products, including the new wireless voice *Dictation 150* headset, into the medical and legal markets.

To contribute to the MediView marketing campaign, you will be assigned some medical and dental market research to complete, you will continue to learn specialized medical and legal vocabulary, and you will be assigned to write several documents aimed at assisting medical and legal customers.

section 4

Speaking Solutions in the Medical Market

Are you ready to work at MediView? Starting a new job can be intimidating. Everything is new. Even the language people speak is loaded with complex technical terms you probably haven't heard before. But don't worry. You were hired because you have the skills and abilities your company is looking for. And every company knows it must help train its employees in its shoptalk and its products and procedures.

In the activities that follow, you will be given several assignments that will help you understand MediView's customers and the products it sells. As a member of the MediView office team, you will help sell MediView products into the rapidly expanding medical and dental markets. To sell in these markets, the MediView sales and marketing teams must communicate effectively with doctors, nurses, dentists, and other medical professionals. This means learning their vocabulary, acronyms, technical terms, and what their needs are. Medical sales and marketing is a complex field that requires training and hands-on experience.

In your new position, you will be assigned some medical and dental market research to complete. You will compile information, prepare vocabulary lists and training information for sales representatives, and write a press release targeted at medical customers. So let's start, because there's plenty of work to be done!

Activity 5

Training the Team in Medical Terminology

OBJECTIVES: In this activity you will...

(A) Research and dictate medical definitions and terminology

(B) Record a variety of new medical terms

(C) Test your dictation speed and accuracy

Congratulations! You're the newest employee at MediView. After a few days of employee orientation, you're ready to take on some actual medical marketing office assignments. In the *Say This!* section, your new manager, Angie Harrington, will explain one of the assignments you will be completing in the *Tackle These Terms* section.

Say This!

1. Dictate the following instructions from your manager which explain the purpose behind the *Tackle These Terms* section that follows:

   "Welcome! I'm very glad you are working at MediView. As my marketing assistant, you will help me in many ways. One of your assignments is to research medical and dental terminology. You must also communicate this information to our medical sales representatives around the country.

   "Our sales team works with medical professionals. However, most of our sales representatives are fresh out of business school and have no medical training. To help them prepare, we send daily email explaining our products and providing information about the medical professionals and organizations we are targeting. I have some important information that I need you to dictate for our medical sales team today!"

2. Correct and train any words you may have misspoken.

3. How close are you to dictating 140 words per minute? It's fun to know approximately how fast you are dictating. The two paragraphs contain approximately 700 characters. Dictate the paragraphs again while timing yourself. If you dictate both paragraphs in less than one minute, you are speaking faster than 140 words per minute. However, remember that accuracy is more important than speed. Dictating at 110 words per minute with few errors is better than making lots of mistakes at 150 words per minute. Adjust your speed to improve your accuracy!

4. Save a final copy of both paragraphs as **Instructions**.

Tackle These Terms

The major speech recognition software programs offer specialized medical vocabularies that can be purchased and installed into your speech recognition software. Using these additional medical vocabulary tools will dramatically increase your recognition accuracy when you speak difficult medical terms. However, if you're using a version of your speech software designed for normal dictation, your accuracy will decline dramatically when dictating technical medical terms, so you will need to train many of them. If you train these terms, you can expect 90–100 percent accuracy thereafter.

1. Here is a list of today's terms. Dictate this list of terms first and train any words your software does not understand. Use the pronunciation guide to help you say any words that are new to you.

Terms	Pronunciation
Anesthesiology	an – es – thee – ze – ol – o – gee
Cardiology	car – dee – ol – o – gee
Chiropractic	kai – row – prak – tik
Cosmetic Surgery	cause – meh – tik
Dermatology	der – ma – tol – o – gee
Endocrinology	end – o – krin – ol – o – gee
Gerontology	jer – on – tol – o – gee
Immunology	im – you – nol – o – gee
Neurology	new – rol – o – gee
Ophthalmology	off –thal – mol – o – gee

2. Dictate the list of terms again along with their corresponding definitions, filling in the blank lines with the proper terms.

_____– concerned with the physiological needs of patients, including structural, spinal, musculoskeletal, neurological, and vascular health.

_____– the study of glands and hormone disorders in the human body.

_____– concerned with the treatment of the eye, including the anatomy, function, and pathology of the eye.

_____ – the practice of medicine dedicated to the relief of pain and total care of the surgical patient before, during and after surgery.

_____– the study of aging and its biological, psychological, and sociological impacts.

_____ – often called plastic surgery. Concerns itself with such procedures as face-lifts, hair replacements, face implants, liposuction, nose surgery, tummy tucks, and even tattoo removal.

_____ – the study of the structure and function of the immune system, human immunity, and the interaction of antigens with specific antibodies.

_____ – the diagnosis and treatment of heart and circulatory disease.

_____ – works with brain and nervous disorders including such things as ALS (Lou Gehrig's disease), Alzheimer's, brain surgery, cerebral palsy, epilepsy, head and brain injury, headaches, Huntington's disease, migraines, multiple sclerosis, muscular dystrophy, neurological tumors, Parkinson's disease, spinal injuries, and stroke.

_____ – study of the physiology and pathology of the skin and the treatment of skin disorders such as acne and melanoma.

3. Use your copy-and-paste skills to arrange this list of definitions in alphabetical order.

4. You will also copy and paste these definitions to another document in the next activity, so save them carefully as **Tackle These Terms 1**.

F Y I You can check your answers on the **www.speakingabout.com** web site. Click the link for your specific speech recognition product and then choose the link called **Speaking About... Tackle These Terms**.

Activity 6 | *Training the Medical Sales Team*

OBJECTIVES In this activity you will...

(A) Dictate an email update to the medical sales team

(B) Dictate medical definitions, terminology, and procedures

(C) Dictate an email message of your own

Keeping the sales team trained and informed about new MediView products is a major challenge, but daily email updates help the sales team stay informed. In this exercise you will dictate an email update to the sales team while learning a great deal about a specific medical product: tracheotomy tubes.

Say This!

1. Dictate the email message shown on the next page from Angie to the sales team. The first part defines a new product that MediView is marketing and selling to medical clients. The second part requires you to copy and paste the **Tackle These Terms 1** definitions from the previous activity to the end of your message (or create an email attachment). If possible, use your voice skills to accomplish this copy-and-paste or attachment routine without using your mouse or the keyboard.

 Tracheotomy is pronounced **tray – key – ott – o – me**. Trachea is said **tray – key – uh**.

FROM: AngieH@corpview.com

TO: MediView_Sales@corpview.com

SUBJECT: The Product Update of the Day!

TODAY'S FEATURED PRODUCT: TRACHEOTOMY TUBES

The trachea is the tube (often called the windpipe) running from the larynx (also called the voice box) down the neck where it divides to form the two bronchial tubes into the lungs. If the windpipe is blocked, preventing the patient from breathing, a tracheotomy is performed. This procedure involves the insertion of a tube through a surgical opening in the trachea. A tracheotomy tube maintains an open air passage.

MediView markets and sells tracheotomy tubes that are easily attached using Velcro straps that hold the tubes in place around the neck of the patient. Our tracheotomy tubes can be positioned quickly and will reliably perform their life-saving function even while the patient is being moved from the scene of an accident to a medical facility.

Our tracheotomy tubes are sold in packages of 24 in the following sizes:

Part Number	Size	Neck Measurement
T017	Infant	Neck size 6–8 inches
T027	Small (pediatric)	Neck size 8–12 inches
T037	Medium	Neck size 12–16 inches
T047	Large	Neck size 16–20 inches
T057	Extra large	Neck size 20–24 inches

We have a goal to sell 5,000 cases of tracheotomy tubes during this fiscal year. We are 14 percent on the way to our goal. Please focus your energies on emergency room, paramedics, and other emergency care professionals and facilities.

Starting with this message, we are adding a new feature called "Tackle These Terms" to our daily updates. This feature will help you learn specialized medical vocabulary. If you encounter any terms you don't understand, feel free to email our newly hired marketing assistant, [insert your name], who has the assignment to research these terms for you.

Good luck on your quarterly sales goals!

Sincerely,

Angie Harrington

Marketing and Sales Director

MediView Division

Attachment: Tackle These Terms 1

2. Save your work as **Product Update 1**.

Speak for Yourself!

Now that you have dictated your first *Product Update of the Day!* email message, start preparing a message for tomorrow's delivery. Your first email update discussed the tracheotomy procedure. Research and prepare a similar message concerning another medical condition, Carpal Tunnel Syndrome or CTS.

In the activities that follow, MediView will be promoting its new wireless dictation headset called the *Dictation 150*. This product can help reduce CTS among medical and dental professionals. Go online and research CTS. Visit the **speakingabout.com** web site and click on the link called **Speaking About Carpal Tunnel and RSI**. Select one or more of the online articles and use the information to prepare an informative update for the medical sales team. Limit the length of your email to 250-400 words.

Save your summary as **Carpal Tunnel**.

Print your **Carpal Tunnel** and **Product Update 1** documents and proofread them. Use your proofreaders' symbols to mark errors. Make corrections and resave your documents.

Activity 7 | *Researching the Dental Market*

OBJECTIVES   In this activity you will...

Speaking About... Précis and Executive Summaries

(A) Dictate an executive summary from a dental journal article

(B) Dictate medical definitions and terminology

(C) Dictate another executive summary

Angie will explain a new product that you have been assigned to work with in the *Think Before You Speak* section. But first, take a few minutes and learn an important summarizing technique that will have you taking great voice-dictation notes in no time.

⟹ ## Speaking About...

Précis and Executive Summaries

Speaking Solutions in This Activity...

Learn to voice-summarize

A *précis* is a concise summary of the main points contained in a journal article, magazine article, or chapter in a textbook. Office professionals often use this summarizing technique to create executive summaries. An *executive summary* is a concise statement summarizing the contents of a larger document.

These brief summaries come in very handy. They are often requested by decision makers who are often too busy to read lengthy articles themselves, but still need to know the key points and main ideas.

Follow these steps:

a. Begin with a specific goal in mind. (In this case, you will summarize a discussion from Angie Harrington, your manager, and later you will summarize a lengthy article and prepare an executive summary of its contents for her.)

b. Read the entire article, discussion, or selection first.

c. Read the selection a second time with your speech recognition microphone handy. Look for and dictate each main idea and major heading and subheading as you read. (Headings signal to the reader any new topics contained in the article.)

d. Look for the topic sentences in each paragraph. Dictate any important topic sentences. A topic sentence summarizes the core or main idea of the paragraph.

e. Continue speaking in complete sentences.

f. Go back through your work and correct it so it reads smoothly. You can print out a copy, mark the mistakes, and enter these corrections.

We will give you an example before you start: an excerpt from an online dental article. We have placed in bold letters the parts of the excerpt that you might dictate.

Say This!

1. Try the following example. The key ideas are marked in bold letters. Only dictate the key ideas, inserting the needed punctuation as you speak to create complete sentences:

The Dreaded Periodontal Exam

In the complex world of voice-related software, a single example can illuminate the implications of speech recognition in surprisingly simple terms. For instance, take the dreaded periodontal exam.

In this soft tissue examination, the dentist or dental **hygienist probes with a sharp instrument deep into a patient's gums**—several times in fact. Probes are made into various portions of the gums **looking for signs of gum disease. It's a slow process** because the results of **each probe must be meticulously recorded** by the hygienist. This requires stopping and starting the exam over and over again. Ouch!

F Y I In this example you would simply dictate the following while adding the required punctuation to make the summary clear. For example:

The Dreaded Periodontal Exam: In this soft tissue examination, the dentist or hygienist probes with a sharp instrument deep into a patient's gums looking for signs of gum disease. It's a slow process. Each probe must be meticulously recorded.

2. Save this as **Periodontal** before moving to the next section.

Think Before You Speak...

1. Read the entire discussion from Angie on the page shown below before you start to dictate it. Read the discussion a second time with your speech recognition microphone handy. Look for and dictate each main idea. Reduce the entire discussion down to less than 150 words, but with no loss in meaning. Less than100 words would be even better!

Angie: "Conducting the dreaded periodontal exam using speech recognition technology requires the use of a wireless dictation headset. Dictation headsets with wires may accidentally touch the patient, creating a biohazard. Anytime a medical or dental piece of equipment comes into contact with a patient it must be sterilized or thrown away. Fortunately, MediView has a new wireless headset that is perfect for conducting this essential dental examination.

"Several years ago, in 1997 to be exact, the Research and Development team in the TeleView division of Corporate View conducted a study of speech recognition headsets. You can find copies of their research on our corporate Intranet site. Basically, they found that the long extension cords going from the headsets to the computers were constantly getting in the way. Books and reports would be placed on the cords. The cords didn't allow mobility for users to move about the room, and they were constantly being tangled up with mouse cords and other wires found on computers. Everything became a tangled mess.

"In response, TeleView engineers developed a wireless microphone headset that could be used anywhere within 100 feet of a computer to dictate text and data into a computer. This microphone headset has sold well in the consumer computer market, particularly among customers who are concerned about carpal tunnel injuries.

"We have been asked to sell this product into the medical, dental, and legal markets. The headset microphone is called the *Dictation 150.* We think there is a huge market among medical office assistants, nurses, doctors, dental hygienists, speech-language pathologists and other related occupations.

"The medical and dental markets are particularly interesting. Medical and dental practitioners, such as registered nurses and dental hygienists, can't use speech recognition headsets with cords very effectively. A traditional headset with its long cord can't come into contact with the patient without creating a biohazard. The wireless solution is ideal and is being used more and more.

"As I mentioned earlier, in medical and dental offices, where biohazards exist, if any headset becomes contaminated while working with the patient, the headset must be sterilized properly or disposed of entirely. The TeleView technicians have developed an inexpensive wireless microphone headset that can be used once and thrown away at minimal cost of under $10.00 per set. While there are many other wireless headsets on the market, we believe that our headset, for the cost, provides the highest level of audio input quality and is ideal for data entry in ambulatory care settings and in medical and dental offices.

"We need you to research and build a business case for this new and exciting product before we go to market!"

2. Save your summary as **Executive Summary 1.**

Speak for Yourself! (Online)

1. Go to **www.speakingabout.com.** As the site opens, select the product you are using and click **Speaking About... The Medical World.**

2. You need to summarize the article "It's the Talk of the Medical World." Start by reading the entire article first, then summarize it section by section. Summarize with complete sentences. You may need to train some of the words like *hygienist, transcriptionists,* and *periodontal,* and phrases like *Henry Schein* and *Dentrix Dental Systems.* **NOTE:** Henry Schein is a major competitor of MediView.

3. After you have finished summarizing, save your document as **Executive Summary 2.**

4. Review your entire summary, then proofread and edit it. Reduce your entire summary to 350 words or less. Edit any part of your abbreviated executive summary document that needs improvement.

5. Format the document using the report format you learned in the *Speaking About... Reports* section of Lesson 10.

Tackle These Terms

Before the sales team can effectively sell to the dental industry, they must know exactly who are the potential customers for the new *Dictation 150 Wireless Headset* in the dental field. A list of terms and occupations will help the sales team learn to whom they will be selling the *Dictation 150* in the future.

1. Dictate the following list of terms first, and train any new words your software does not understand. Pronunciation tips are provided for terms that may not be commonly known.

Terms	Pronunciation
Dental Assistant	
Dental Laboratory Technician	
Dentist	
Gingivitis	gin – ji – vai – tus
Hygienist	hi – jen – ist
Periodontal Exam	pear – ee – o – don – tal
Periodontist	pear – ee – o – don – tist
Office Manager	

2. Dictate the list of terms again with their definitions, filling in the blank lines with the correct terms.

_____ – a highly trained professional concerned with healthy teeth and gum diseases. There were more than 152,000 of these professionals in the U.S. in 1996.

_____ – a dentist specializing in the treatment of gum disease.

_____ – a specialized examination of the gums to help identify gum disease.

_____ – dental assistant who cleans teeth, educates patients in dental health, administers local anesthetic, and performs periodontal scaling.

_____ – inflammation of the gums. A first sign of periodontal (gum) disease.

_____ – will assist dentists with patient care and perform X rays and routine dental procedures, such as taking impressions and sterilizing equipment.

_____ – receives customers, schedules appointments, and manages the dental office. Must be a trained office professional and computer specialist. Speech recognition training is becoming increasingly vital. A bookkeeping background is usually required.

_____ – may perform dental research or manufacture crowns, braces, and dentures based upon impressions of the patient's mouth taken by the dentist or dental assistant.

3. Save these terms as **Tackle These Terms 2**.

NOTE: You can check your answers on the **speakingabout.com** web site. Click the link for your specific product and then choose the link called **Speaking About... Tackle These Terms.**

Activity 8 | *Preparing a Press Release for Medical/ Dental Professionals*

OBJECTIVES In this activity you will...

Speaking About... Press Releases

(A) Dictate a press release announcing a new medical product

(B) Prepare a press release of your own

(C) Dictate medical definitions and terminology

One of the essential tasks marketing assistants perform is to help prepare press releases for the media. Press releases help announce new products and can provide free advertising and media hype for new corporate initiatives.

Before you dictate your first press release in the *Say This!* section, review how they are written in *Speaking About... Press Releases* below.

Speaking About...

Press Releases

Speaking Solutions in This Activity...

Apply the basics of writing press releases

Although you are trying to present your product in the best light possible, you have to do it carefully. Keep your wording as simple and neutral as possible. Your release should never read like glitzy ad copy. Instead, it should have an almost "down-home," conversational flavor. You can do this by observing the following guidelines:

- *Use short sentences.* Use short sentences to present your information clearly and simply: Avoid sentences more than 25 words long. Use many simple sentences instead of overly complex compound sentences. Unless your audience includes high-tech readers, don't sound too high-tech or technical.

- *Keep paragraphs short.* A paragraph should rarely be longer than five or six lines or longer than two or three sentences.

- *Use verbs liberally and adjectives sparingly.* Verbs are power words. Use them to tell what a product can do. Too many adjectives add unnecessary fluff and tend to make the document read like an advertisement.

- *Make the tone neutral.* The tone is the mood of the document. How does it feel when you read it? The reader should feel that the information is being presented in an unbiased way. There should never be a feeling of hyperbole or overstatement.

Say This!

1. Dictate the press release shown below. You may need to train some of the words like *headsets* and *wireless*. You may wish to train *Dictation 150 Wireless Headset* as a phrase. Try the following:

PRESS RELEASE

August 9, 2002

Contact: Maria Bravo
MediView
One Corporate View Drive
Boulder, Colorado 80303-0103
Phone: (303) 555-0110
Email: mbravo@corpview.com

MediView Participates in Speech-Language Pathology Conference

BOULDER, COLORADO, August 9, 2002. MediView is pleased to announce its participation in the American Speech-Language-Hearing Association (ASHA) conference in Austin, Texas. ASHA represents over 96,000 speech-language pathologists. These speech-language professionals treat speech, language, communication, voice, and other related disorders. They work with people who cannot make speech sounds or who cannot speak clearly and effortlessly. This includes conditions like stuttering or the inability to speak caused by stroke, cerebral palsy, hearing loss, or brain injury. Speech recognition technology is often used to help individuals learn to speak or to speak more clearly.   Such computer-based training requires the use of high-quality microphone headsets.

MediView, a manufacturer of speech technology, will be unveiling its new *Dictation 150 Wireless Headset* at the ASHA conference for the first time. MediView's interest in speech-language pathology began during the testing of this new product. The *Dictation 150* was tested with many individuals whose physical handicaps prevented them from using headsets with long extension cords, such as people confined to wheelchairs or hospital beds. Wires dangling between the computer and the speech-language pathology patient often created a biohazard and become entangled in other life support devices. The *Dictation 150 Wireless Headset* allows speech-language pathology professionals to continue working with patients despite extreme limitations in personal mobility.

MediView will be unveiling its new technology in its trade show booth at the annual ASHA conference. The *Dictation 150 Wireless Headset* has been thoroughly tested in other medical and dental offices as well. Its first office trial was with dental hygienists conducting periodontal exams. The *Dictation 150 Wireless Headset* has an effective range of over 100 feet. It has exceptional audio reception qualities that make it ideal for speech-language pathology patients.

Anticipated Product Release Date: September 1, 2002

###

2. Save your document as **Press Release**.

Dictate the Definitions

Knowing the shoptalk for the industry in which you are working is vital. Dictate the following terms. you may need to train such terms as *PPE*, *eyewash*, and *biohazardous*. Save this list as **More Medical Definitions**.

Transcriptionist – efficient typist who traditionally converted recorded dictation from doctors into meaningful medical records, reports, and summaries. Increasingly, this task has become automated through the use of speech recognition software. These professionals today must be capable of editing speech-to-text, computer-generated transcriptions to ensure their accuracy. This requires a deep knowledge of medical terminology.

Barrier – obstacle that exists to protect an individual from contact with blood or other potentially infectious materials. Called personal protective equipment (PPE), barriers include gloves, masks, face shields, laboratory coats, protective eye wear, and gowns.*

Work practice controls – measures used in the workplace that consist of physical equipment and mechanical devices to control employee exposure to blood-borne pathogens and other potentially infectious materials. Examples are sharps disposable containers, hand washing facilities, PPE, eyewash stations, and so on.**

Universal precautions – guidelines established by the Centers for Disease Control (CDC) for the protection of the health care workers from infectious diseases.***

Spill kit – commercially packaged materials containing supplies and equipment needed to clean up a spill of a biohazardous substance.****

Speak for Yourself!

After dictating a press release, you now have some idea about how they're written. Prepare a press release about a new product just coming to market or, if you get stuck for an idea, create a press release about you! Be creative. Announce important things about your new product, or highlight things that are going on in your life and in your career.

Save your press release as **My Press Release**.

Print both **Press Release** and **My Press Release** and proofread them. Use your proofreaders' symbols to mark errors. Make corrections and resave your documents.

*From Wilburta Lindh et al., *Comprehensive Medical Assisting*. (Albany, NY: Delmar/Thomson Learning, 1998), G-3.
**Ibid., G-25.
***Ibid., G-24.
****Ibid., G-22.

section 5

Speaking Solutions in the Legal Market

The medical and legal fields share something in common: accurate records are critical in both professions. Medical institutions are legally responsible for maintaining clear and concise records of their interactions with patients. Failure to do so can bring legal actions against them from a variety of government agencies, insurance companies, and individuals who feel they have been wronged. The medical profession is awash in paperwork.

In like manner, the legal field is a sea of documents. Legal teams prepare motions, briefs, contracts, interrogatories, partnership agreements, opinions, subpoenas, petitions, legislation, and a host of other documents. Charles Cooper, an attorney at Corporate View, might sum it up this way: "The fact that you often find so many legal books and case files around a legal office provides a clue to the kind of work lawyers spend most of their time doing. Lawyers work with laws, and laws take the form of written documents."

With so many written documents to create, is it any wonder that speech recognition is catching on in the legal market?

Because Corporate View doesn't have a marketing and sales team that specifically sells its products in the legal market, they have asked MediView to form a special market research team to investigate marketing and selling the *Dictation 150 Wireless Headset* to legal professionals. As the marketing assistant, your next job is to help investigate the legal market.

Activity 9 | *Emailing for Legal Advice*

OBJECTIVES   In this activity you will...

(A) Dictate an email message of inquiry about the legal market

(B) Dictate an email message of your own

(C) Dictate legal definitions and terminology

Speaking About... Capitalizing Letters in Titles (Online)

In 1996, three employees were awarded a $6,000,000 jury verdict against Digital Equipment Corporation because they acquired repetitive strain injuries (RSI) and carpal tunnel syndrome (CTS) from using their company's keyboards on the job. This was the first major award of its kind for keyboard-related injuries.

Given the amount of paperwork that legal professionals must generate, they must be especially concerned about minimizing computer-related injuries. Obviously, speech recognition can help reduce cases of RSI and CTS in the legal field.

Chances are, you don't know too much about legal careers, legal organizations, legal offices, or the type of paperwork they must do. Most people don't. In order to prepare to market the *Dictation 150* wireless headset to this demographic population, you must learn who your legal customers are and how you can advertise to them. You must also learn their vocabulary. Just as the medical profession has its shop talk, so it is with the legal profession.

Fortunately, you don't need to look any further than the Legal Services department at Corporate View for advice. Major corporations employ legal teams to look out for their corporate interests. Corporate View's legal office is similar to other such legal offices found in corporations all over the world. An email interview to Charles Cooper, an attorney on the Legal Services team, may generate the type of information you will need to know.

Say This!

1. Dictate the email message as shown below to Charles Cooper, an attorney in the Corporate View Legal Services department. You may need to train a few words.

To: CharlesCooper@corpview.com
From: *<Insert your email address>*
Date: *<Insert today's date>*
Subject: The Legal Market
Message:

Dear Mr. Cooper:

I was given your name as a possible resource. I am part of the MediView marketing team that has just been assigned the responsibility to sell the *Dictation 150* wireless headset to legal professionals. Because Corporate View does not have a legal marketing team, we have been asked to research the profit potential of selling the *Dictation 150* headset (designed for the medical market) to legal office professionals. I have a series of questions that I hope you can help me answer:

1. What types of jobs are found in a typical legal office? What kind of law do you specialize in?

2. What do you believe will be the response from the legal community about using our wireless dictation headset in the legal office?

3. What are some of the organizations and associations that legal professionals join? (And do any of them allow advertisements on their web sites? In what ways can we market and advertise to legal professionals?)

4. What types of dictation tasks are performed in a legal office that would make effective sales demonstrations for the *Dictation 150* headset?

Thank you for taking the time to answer these questions.

Sincerely,

<Insert your name>

2. Save this email message as **Sample Email**.

Tackle These Terms

While you are waiting for an email reply from Charles Cooper, tackle a few legal terms. If you learn the legal shoptalk, you will have greater success making a profit in the legal market. You need to train, record, and dictate some legal terms and their definitions.

1. Dictate the following list of legal terms and train any words your software does not understand, such as *paraprofessional* and *paralegal*. Pronunciation tips are provided for terms that may not be commonly known. Save your file as **Legal Definitions**.

Terms	Pronunciation
Antitrust legislation	an – tie – trust
Attorney	
Contract	
Interrogatories	in – tear – og – ah –tor – ees
Legal Office Assistant	
Legal Receptionist	
Motion	
Office Administrator	
Paralegal	pair – ah – lee – gul
Subpoena	suh –peen – ah

2. Dictate the list of terms again along with their corresponding definitions, filling in the blank lines with the proper term. **NOTE:** Asterisks after some of the definitions indicate source references at the bottom of the page. Do not speak the asterisks.

_____ – a person legally licensed and authorized to represent other persons or to transact business on their behalf as their legal agent.

_____ – a person responsible for the business administration of a legal office. Usually responsible for such mission-critical functions as the management of human resources, finance and accounting, marketing, and sales. Usually holds a degree in law or business office management, finance and accounting, or human resource management.

_____ – a person who provides assistance to lawyers. Highly trained in legal terminology. Must be able to correspond effectively in written legal communications. Traditionally referred to as a legal secretary.

_____ – a "front desk" person whose responsibility is to greet telephone callers, visitors, or clients.

_____ – a paraprofessional that assists attorneys. Must be trained in the law and in legal processes.

_____ – laws opposed to trusts, or illegal combinations and monopolies, which restrict fair trade and prohibit competitive business practices.

_____ – a written order commanding a person to appear in court under penalty of law.

_____ – a petition to the court for an order directing some act.*

_____ – a pretrial discovery tool consisting of a set of questions propounded to a party.* *(Propound* means to offer for discussion.)

_____ – an agreement that creates legal and enforceable obligations binding each party.**

3. Use your copy and paste skills to arrange this list of definitions in alphabetical order.

4. You will also copy and paste these definitions to another document in the next activity, so save them carefully as **Tackle These Terms 3**.

NOTE: You can check your answers on the **speakingabout.com** web site. Click the link for your specific speech recognition product, and then choose the link called **Speaking About... Tackle These Terms.**

Speak for Yourself!

Email is one of the most common forms of interoffice communication. However, you should always remember that email is never private. An email you send to someone in confidence may actually be forwarded to many other people. Corporate email has been used as evidence in court cases, too, such as in the antitrust case against Microsoft. Email may be used against you in a court of law, so don't write anything in an email message that you don't want the world to know about!

Remember these rules when composing your email messages:

- Enter email addresses carefully
- Use a descriptive subject line and capitalize it as a heading (*see next section*)
- Keep email short and concise
- Proofread your message before sending
- Keep your email on a professional level

*From Robert Cummins, *Legal Office: Concepts and Procedures*. (Cincinnati: South-Western Educational Publishing, 1998), 301.
**Ibid., 298.

Email is one of the most efficient uses of speech recognition. With a keyboard, average office employees can spend hours responding to their email. With speech recognition, office workers can dispatch their email more quickly and efficiently. See for yourself: Take a few minutes to voice-type an email to a friend. Save the message portion in a file called **My Email**.

 F Y I Some speech programs will allow you to dictate directly into your email program. Depending on your software, you may need to a transfer or copy and paste your email message from your speech recognition software to your email program.

Speaking About...

Capitalizing Letters in Titles (Online)

 As an office professional, you must capitalize titles properly. The same rules apply for subject lines in email messages or headings in reports. For a brief review of this critical skill, visit **www.speakingabout.com**. As the site opens, select the title of the book you are using and click **Speaking About... Capitalizing Letters in Titles**. Follow the online instructions.

Activity 10 | *Dictating a Memo from an Attorney*

OBJECTIVES In this activity you will...

Speaking About... Confusing Terms 2

(A) Dictate an attorney's memo from handwritten notes

(B) Dictate a memo of your own

(C) Dictate information about professional legal and medical organizations

Analyzing the types of customers typically found in a legal office will be much easier with the help of the Legal Services team. Charles Cooper replied with handwritten answers that he jotted down on a notepad while flying from Denver to Cincinnati on company business. He has asked you to clean up and proofread his notes and format them in a memo before sharing the information with others on your market research team.

You will notice many mistakes in Mr. Cooper's notes. Most of them are misused or confusing words. Since you know that there is no relationship between intelligence and poor spelling skills, you can chuckle about it. However, the document needs proofreading. To protect Mr. Cooper's grammatical reputation, you should correct the mistakes for him. But first, read *Speaking About... Confusing Terms 2* below to make sure you catch each error!

Speaking About...

Confusing Terms 2

Speaking Solutions in This Activity...

A. Choose properly between the words *it's* and *its*

B. Choose properly between the words *there*, *their*, and *they're*

C. Choose properly between the words *accept* and *except*

D. Choose properly between the words *too*, *to*, and *two*

As you dictate the handwritten notes in the *Say This!* section, you must make a decision between certain confusing words that sound the same, but have different meanings, such as those listed above. Make your word choices based upon the following rules. As you review the rules, try dictating the examples:

A. Choose properly between the words *it's* and *its*

- *It's* is a contraction meaning *it is* (or sometimes *it has*).

  It's important to check the accuracy of legal documents.
  It is important to check the accuracy of legal documents.

  It's a fine cutthroat trout.
  It is a fine cutthroat trout.

- *Its* is a possessive pronoun (like *their*, *his*, *her*) indicating ownership.

  The legal reference manual was posted to its web site.
  The law firm won its first major court case.

B. Choose properly between the words *there*, *their*, and *they're*

- *There* indicates, identifies, or points out a thing or a place.

  Look over there.
  There is a large fish in the river.

- *Their* is a possessive pronoun (like *its*, *her*, *his*, *our*) indicating ownership.

  Their snowboarding skills have improved.
  The hockey team gave it their best.

- *They're* is a contraction meaning *they are*.

  They're going to write a business plan.
  When they're working, the job gets done.

C. Choose properly between the words *accept* and *except*

- *Accept* is a verb which means *to say yes*, *to take*, *to receive*, or *to respond favorably to*.

- *Except* is a preposition which means *leaving out* or *excluding*.

  Carl accepted the award from the business teachers.
  Everyone attended except Dave and Mark.

  The teachers accepted his advice.
  All department chairs were there except Karen.

D. Choose properly between the words *too*, *to*, and *two*

- *Too* is an adverb which means *excessively*; it also means *also*.

  I had too much to eat.
  Mary found writing the business plan too difficult.
  I wanted to catch a bass, too.
  The ski trip was too expensive.

- *To* is a preposition.

  Bill is going to ski.
  Please listen to our message.
  The motives of those to whom we speak are pure.

- *Two* is the number 2.

I want two boys and two girls to stay after school.
The two of us wrote the proposal.

Save your work as **Confusing 2**.

Think Before You Speak...

Choose the correct form of the word in parentheses in each sentence. Add and save these sentences to your **Confusing 2** file.

The cat wanted (it's *or* its) **box.**

(It's *or* Its) **going to be a great day for fishing.**

Every plant has (it's *or* its) **own characteristics.**

(It's *or* Its) **nothing against you personally.**

(Their, There, *or* They're) **is nothing better than a hot breakfast.**

The students and (their, there, *or* they're) **parents will attend the show.**

Put the hamster cage over (their, there, *or* they're).

(Their, There, *or* They're) **not concentrating today.**

Please (accept *or* except) **my humble apologies.**

The flowers were all dead (accept *or* except) **one.**

I proposed with the idea that she would (accept *or* except).

(Accept *or* Except) **perhaps Yolanda, they should all be here.**

He couldn't help but smile as he looked into (their, there, *or* they're) **faces.**

(Its *or* It's) **the thought that counts.**

You must (accept *or* except) **responsibility.**

The girls are always washing (their, there, *or* they're) **hands.**

Everyone has one (accept *or* except) **me.**

(Its *or* It's) **rooms were empty and** (its *or* it's) **paint was peeling.**

(Their, There, *or* They're) **is no excuse for wastefulness.**

When will we get (their, there, *or* they're)?

I'm going (too, to, *or* two).

We have (too, to, *or* two) **copies of the business plan; I need them** (too, to, *or* two).

(Too, To, *or* Two) **eat** (too, to, *or* two) **pieces of pie is** (too, to, *or* two) **much for me.**

(Too, To, *or* Two) **days were** (too, to, *or* two) **much for an intern who was** (too, to, *or* two) **sleepy to get to the bottom of the problem.**

Double-check your answers on the Web at **www.speakingabout.com**. As the site opens, select your book or specific speech software program and then click the **Student Answers** link.

Say This!

1. Decipher and dictate the notes on the next page and place them in a memo format. You may need to train a few words, and you will definitely need to fix some mistakes! There are nearly a dozen obviously confusing word errors. Can you correct them? Refer back to the *Speaking About... Confusing Terms 2* section on page 5-7 if you have questions about some of the words.

MEMO

Too: **The Legal Marketing Research Team**

From: **Charles Cooper**

Date: *<Dictate the current date>*

Subject: **The Legal Office Market**

Question 1: What types of jobs are found in a typical legal office? What kind of law do you specialize in?

The typical legal office will employ attorneys, office administrators, legal office assistants, receptionists, law clerks, paralegals, and legal investigators. In large firms their are also accountants and bookkeepers. Each of these positions could make use of the new Dictation 150 Wireless Headset.

Working for Corporate View, I specialize in corporate law. I wrote a training article for HR one day on corporate law. Let me find that document and send it two you later. Look for it tomorrow.

Question 2: What do you believe will be the response from the legal community about using our wireless dictation headset in the legal office?

Its exciting that MediView is going after the legal office market. Theyre response should be very positive about the Dictation 150. Even though this represents a new market for our company, I think we can be successful marketing and selling this product to legal professionals. The medical evidence concerning the link between keyboards and CTS and RSI is overwhelming. An increasing number of Worker's Compensation claims and related legal cases has demonstrated the need to except changes in the way employees work with their computers. Keyboard injuries impact every industry, not just the medical and legal professions.

I have used speech recognition myself since 1997. I see other attorneys and legal office workers except the technology every day. They all appreciate quality speech recognition equipment. The Dictation 150 is the most accurate headset I have ever used.

The Dictation 150 solves too of my major frustrations. First, most of the headsets I have used have long dangling cords that get in the way. Its a hassle to untangle these cords. Second, I dont like to be confined to my chair when I dictate. With the Dictation 150 I can be anywhere within 100 feet of my computer and still dictate. I believe most legal office professionals want to move around their offices and dont want to be restricted by the length of their microphone cords.

Question 3: What are some of the organizations and associations that legal professionals join? (And do any of them allow advertisements on their web sites? In what ways can we market and advertise to legal professionals?)

- American Bar Association (ABA)
- Association of Legal Administrators (ALA)
- National Association of Legal Secretaries (NALS)

I dont believe any of these associations allow advertising on their web sites, but some have magazine publications that take ads. Also, each association sponsors conventions and conferences with showrooms where vendors and suppliers demonstrate a wide assortment of legal products and services. Have you considered demonstrating at these conferences? They are quite popular.

Question 4: What types of dictation tasks are performed in a legal office that would make effective sales demonstrations for the *Dictation 150* headset?

Their are many possible documents that can be dictated during a marketing or sales demonstration; subpoenas, motions, interrogatories, and contracts come to mind. If you go to any conferences, you may want to demonstrate the Dictation 150 using information about the legal association sponsoring the convention or conference. For example, for an ABA conference it might be fun to dictate some of the ethics information published on there web site.

<Insert your initials>

2. Save this file as **Sample Memo**.

Speak for Yourself!

Because of email, memos are not used nearly as much as they used to be. However, they can still be a very effective form of communication. They are particularly valuable as handouts in meetings, and they can be posted on bulletin boards in company break rooms.

Prepare a short 250-word memo describing an upcoming office party or an important business meeting. Attendance is required!

Activity 11 | *Reporting on Contract Law*

OBJECTIVES In this activity you will...

(A) Learn about contract law

(B) Dictate legal terms and definitions

(C) Dictate a report on contract law

Charles Cooper wrote an article explaining contract law. However, the article seems to have a few blanks in it. To prepare to fill in the blanks, train the legal terms in Step 1 of the *Tackle These Terms* section below before you start dictating Mr. Cooper's article.

Tackle These Terms

1. Dictate the following list of legal terms and train any words your software does not understand. Pronunciation tips are provided for terms that may not be commonly known.

Terms	Pronunciation
acceptance	
breach of contract	
comparative negligence	neg – lih – jence
consideration	
contract law	
contributory negligence	neg – lih – jence
culpa lata	cul – pa la – ta
damages	
general counsel	
gross negligence	
lawyer	
litigation	Lih – tih – gay – shun
negligence	neg – lih – jence
offer	
tort	tore – t

2. Dictate the report from Charles Cooper on contract law (shown on the next page), filling in the blank lines with the proper terms as you come to them.

CONTRACT LAW

I am the _____ for Corporate View. This means that I am the senior lawyer for the corporation. I'm a full-time employee, and I spend most of my time working with contract law. I work with eleven other attorneys. A _____ is a person that has been trained and certified in the law to give legal advice and to represent others in _____, which is a formal court action such as a lawsuit. Most of the lawsuits Corporate View faces have to do with contract law.

_____ regulates the enforcement of contracts. This branch of the law is a legal tradition that spans thousands of years and was created by ancient civilizations to support trade. Our contract tradition comes from English law, which is based on old Roman law.

All commercial dealings are based on contracts. Every time you buy a ticket or make a purchase you are participating in a contract. Businesses prepare formal contracts when doing business with each other. Contract law is based upon three principles:

- _____: A proposal which, when accepted, completes a contract, binding both the person making and the person accepting its terms.

- _____: A contract does not go into effect until both parties signify their willingness to agree to the terms of the offer.

- _____: Comes from English law. An 1875 English court decision stated that "some right, interest, profit, or benefit" must come to one or more of the contracting parties. This rule attempts to remove gifts from contract law protections. However, this principle is not always applied.

The failure to fulfill the promise or agreement in a contract is called a _____. The injured party may sue for _____ based on the conditions and terms of the contract. The injured party may sue because of a negligent action. Damages usually take the form of cash payments to offset the loss or suffering caused by the _____. Another name for these cases is _____. This word comes from the Latin word "tortus" which means wrong. There are several kinds of negligence:

- _____ is an action in reckless disregard of the consequences to the wronged party or person. In Latin this level of negligence is called _____, which goes well beyond simple negligence.

- _____ occurs when an act is supported by someone other than the primary defendant but without whose involvement the negligence would not have occurred.

- _____ balances any possible negligence on the part of the victim that may have contributed to the injury. This test is often used to reduce the extent of the damages.

3. Save your report as **Tackle These Terms 4.**

NOTE: You can check your answers on the **speakingabout.com** web site. Click the link for your specific speech recognition product and then choose the link called **Speaking About... Tackle These Terms**.

Dictate the Definitions

Knowing about their professional organizations can help you plan trade show conferences where legal professionals meet to learn how they can do a better job. Demonstrations at these conferences can really showcase the *Dictation 150's* abilities.

1. Dictate the following information about legal organizations. You may need to train some abbreviations such as *ABA*, *ALA*, *NALS*, and *AALNC*.

American Bar Association (ABA) – www.abanet.org – a voluntary association of attorneys to improve legal services.*

Association of Legal Administrators (ALA) – www.alanet.org – an organization that seeks to improve the quality of management in legal services organizations.

Association for Legal Professionals (NALS) – www.nals.org – the largest professional organization for the legal office assistant.**

American Association of Legal Nurse Consultants (AALNC) – www.aalnc.org – an organization dedicated to registered nurses who are consulting in the legal field. Members are involved in legal-medical consulting, medical care issues, and health care law.

2. Save this file as **Legal Organizations**.

Speak for Yourself!

In the *Dictate the Definitions* section you learned about many organizations whose members can benefit from using speech recognition technology. Prepare a short report on how this technology can help lawyers and legal office professionals in their work. This report should be approximately 200–400 words in length.

Save this report as **Why I Use Legal Speech**.

*From Robert Cummins, *Legal Office: Concepts and Procedures*. (Cincinnati: South-Western Educational Publishing, 1998), 295.
**Ibid., 303.

Appendix–Advanced Features

Their are various versions of the award-winning Dragon NaturallySpeaking software. The inexpensive *Essentials* version is not suitable as a learning tool and can't be used to complete the activities in this text. However, the economical *Standard* version accommodates most of the features you will need to be an effective user of speech recognition software. The high-end *Preferred* version of NaturallySpeaking is even more powerful. And there are professional versions, such as the *Medical Suite* and *Legal Suite*, which are customized toward specific professional needs. In this appendix we will cover the following NaturallySpeaking topics. (Sections D and E can be found online at **www.speakingabout.com**.)

- (A) Addressing Trouble Spots
- (B) Improving Recognition Accuracy
- (C) Managing and Expanding Your Vocabulary
- (D) Making Macros
- (E) Manipulating Windows

(A) Addressing Trouble Spots

There are various trouble spots to look out for. For example, what if your computer crashes, destroying your personal NaturallySpeaking profile? And, what if you notice a sudden decline in your recognition accuracy? In this section we will address these and other troubling issues:

- *How to troubleshoot a sudden drop in speech accuracy*
- *How to back up your personal speech profile*
- *How to restore your personal speech profile*

Let's take these problems one at a time:

Troubleshoot a Sudden Drop in Speech Accuracy

Whenever you notice a decline in your ability to dictate, the first possible culprit is your microphone. If the microphone is okay, then check to make sure you are using *your* speech profile. Review these tips:

- Make sure your microphone is plugged in properly. If your headset requires batteries, replace the batteries.
- Run your *Check Audio* utility to recalibrate your audio settings.
- When you're readjusting your audio settings, create a little ambient background noise. Turn the radio or television on in the background. This will force your system to cancel out some of the background noises that may be causing interference.

- Make sure your microphone is in the correct position. Many users think that if they push the microphone as close as possible to their mouths, their accuracy will improve. This, however, usually results in more recognition errors because the microphone begins to pick up your breathing, or even the touch of your lips on the microphone's sponge. Start with the microphone about an inch away from your lower lip or slightly off to the side. As you speak, if lots of extra words appear randomly, move the microphone further away from your mouth. If the microphone can't hear you, move the microphone slightly closer and readjust your audio settings at this adjusted position. Keep your microphone at the same position every time you use NaturallySpeaking.

- Make sure you have selected your own personal speech profile from the **Manage Users** dialog box of the **Users** menu (see Section 1C on your NaturallySpeaking reference card).

- If you feel that your personal speech profile has become corrupted, you should restore your profile (see the next section of this appendix), or delete your user name and re-enroll.

Back Up Your Personal Speech Profile

Be sure to back up your personal speech profile at least once a week. Then, if anything happens to it, you can simply restore your voice data and continue working normally. Follow these steps:

1. Open NaturallySpeaking and choose your personal speech profile.

2. Say or choose *(Click) NaturallySpeaking → Advanced → Backup User*, as shown in Figure A-1. NaturallySpeaking will do the rest. Just wait until NaturallySpeaking has finished backing up your personal voice file.

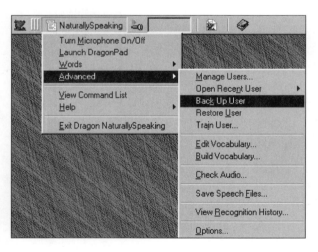

figure A-1

Back Up and Restore your Personal Speech Profile

Restore Your Personal Speech Profile

To restore your personal speech profile, reverse the process as follows:

Say or choose *(Click) NaturallySpeaking → Advanced → Restore User*. NaturallySpeaking will restore your speech profile, saving a copy of your profile and making it available from the **Users** menu.)

Ⓑ Improving Recognition Accuracy

Learning speech recognition software is a constant quest for perfect recognition accuracy. You have probably noticed (it would have been impossible *not* to notice) that after you make changes to your personal speech profile, Dragon asks you if you want to save those changes at the end of the session, as shown in Figure A-2. If you have added a new word to your vocabulary, you should always choose **Yes**, or say *(Click) Yes*, or your improvements will not be saved. Failure to save changes will mean that you will make the same mistakes in the future, never improving your speech profile.

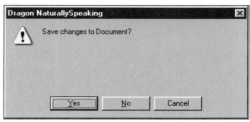

figure A-2
Always Save the Changes to Your Speech Profile

There are other ways to improve your accuracy. In the sections below, we will explain the following:

- *How to add to or redo your enrollment*
- *Why you would read and process additional enrollment stories*
- *How to adjust for different recognition conditions*
- *How to accommodate a new microphone*
- *How to improve your selection and correction technique*

Add to or Redo Your Enrollment

If your personal speech profile is performing well for you, you may be able to improve it even more by adding extra enrollment scripts to NaturallySpeaking.

> **F Y I** For some beginners with less than desirable accuracy, it may be best to simply start over. Why? Through the weeks of practice you have refined your "dictation voice." You probably speak a little differently than you did at the beginning. Re-enrolling or retraining your computer is a good idea for new users. Using your new, refined way of speaking to your computer, redo your enrollment. Speak in the same way as you normally talk your computer.

1. Select your NaturallySpeaking user name before continuing. Add to your enrollment training by selecting *(Click) NaturallySpeaking → Advanced → Train User*, as shown in Figure A-3.

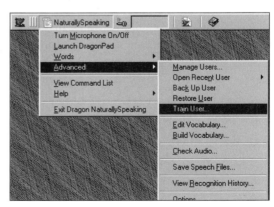

figure A-3
Fine-Tune Your System with the **Train User** Feature

2. Select a story you haven't read previously and read the on-screen instructions. You will be analyzing your voice as directed. (See Figure A-4.) Be sure to speak clearly, using your best dictation voice. Speak the way you intend to talk to your computer in the future. Click **Train Now**, then begin reading aloud.

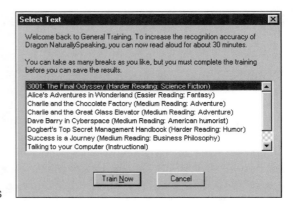

figure A-4

Choose a Story and Read Aloud for About 30 Minutes

Why Read and Process Additional Enrollment Scripts?

The more enrollment scripts you read, the more NaturallySpeaking has to work with as it analyzes your unique way of speaking. Nearly everyone who uses NaturallySpeaking professionally will read about three enrollment scripts eventually. Most report that this does, indeed, improve their speech recognition accuracy. The best advice is to read one enrollment script every few days, at different times of the day, over a period of about a week. This analysis will adjust for the way you change your speaking from day to day and from morning to night.

Adjust for Different Recognition Conditions

You will find yourself dictating in a wide variety of situations with different background noise conditions.

If you find yourself in a noisy environment, the first thing to do is to run your *Check Audio* utility. Run the microphone tuning routine so that you can cancel out any background interference. Saying or choosing *(Click) NaturallySpeaking → Advanced → Check Audio* will do the trick.

If you first enrolled under very quiet conditions, you may want to create a new enrollment under a new name for a noisier condition. For example, if your work environment is much quieter than your home dictation setting, create a separate enrollment under a different name for each environment by selecting the *New* option in the *Manage Users* dialogbox.

This also applies if you are sick. If you have a cold or an abnormally scratchy voice, your recognition accuracy may decline. You can improve your accuracy during this rough spell by running your *Check Audio* utility and creating a new enrollment under a new name, such as **My sick voice**.

 Make sure you back up all of your speech profiles so that your best enrollments are safe and sound!

Accommodate a New Microphone

If you change your microphone, redo your audio settings and create a new enrollment for your new microphone. Different microphones "sound different" to your computer. If you switch microphones, even to a higher quality microphone, your accuracy may actually decline because all of your enrollments have been calculated based upon voice input data from a lower quality device. Therefore, if you notice a decline in performance, you should record a new enrollment with your new microphone.

F Y I   Each dictation microphone has different qualities. Some are more accurate than others! You can use your *Check Audio* utility to compare microphones and test how well a new microphone is working.

Improve Your Selection and Correction Technique

Correcting your mistakes is crucial to improving your recognition accuracy. However, you must remember to use the *Correction* window to correct mistakes, or your corrections will *not* result in improved accuracy. Knowing when to use **Select** or **Choose** inside the *Correction* window is sometimes confusing to new users. It can also be confusing to know when to **Select** or when to use the **Correct** command. Follow these four steps in this order to correct mistakes:

1. Select the error with the **Select <word>** command and then say the correct word. This accomplishes three possible things, all of them helpful in increasing your recognition accuracy:

   - First, when you select an incorrect word and try to say it again, NaturallySpeaking will try to guess the correct form of the word. Who knows, NaturallySpeaking may get it right this time!

   - Second, it gives you a chance to enunciate the word more clearly. After all, most errors are caused by poor or sloppy enunciation.

   - Third, there is a good chance that your new pronunciation of the word, even if it also creates an incorrect word, will result in a closer match to the word you really want, making it easier for NaturallySpeaking to guess the word you will train in the next step.

2. If the word still comes up wrong, use either of these two command sequences to place the word in the **Correction** window:

   Correct <word>

   or

   Select <word>, *Correct That*

3. If the word appears in the selection list, use the **Choose #** command to correct the mistake.

4. If the correct spelling of the word doesn't appear in the selection list, follow these steps:

   a. Spell the word out in the **Correction** window and train it by saying *(Click) Train* or by clicking the **Train** button.

   b. If the correct word appears in your selection list as you are spelling it, use the **Select #** command to select it. Don't finish spelling the word. If you are training *understand*, spell **u n d e . . .**, then as *understand* appears, say **Select 1** or **3**, or whatever number appears next to the correct word. Then say *(Click) Train* or click the **Train** button to train the word.

Poor spellers, listen up! NaturallySpeaking will list problem words in the **Correction** window as you spell them. By watching the **Correction** window's list as you spell, you can make an educated guess as to whether the word is spelled correctly. You can then select the correct word and train it with the assurance that the word has been spelled correctly.

C Managing and Expanding Your Vocabulary

NaturallySpeaking allows you to manage and expand your vocabulary in several ways. In this section we will cover the following:

- *How to remove or retrain words or commands with the* Vocabulary Builder
- *How to use the* Vocabulary Builder

Remove or Retrain Words or Commands with the *Vocabulary Editor*

At times, you may need to delete a word that is causing you grief or that you spelled incorrectly. You can also re-record the pronunciation of a word that doesn't appear properly on your screen after you speak it.

1. Say or choose *(Click) NaturallySpeaking →*
   Advanced → Edit Vocabulary, as shown in
   Figure A-5.

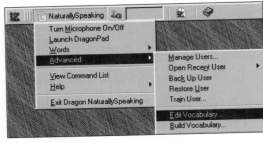

figure A-5

Open the **Vocabulary
Editor** from the
NaturallySpeaking Menu

2. The words appear in alphabetical order
   (see Figure A-6). Choose the word you
   wish to delete or retrain. To retrain a
   word, click the **Train** button or say
   (Click) Train. You can then record the
   word again. To delete a word, choose
   the word to be removed and click the
   Delete button or say *(Click) Delete*.

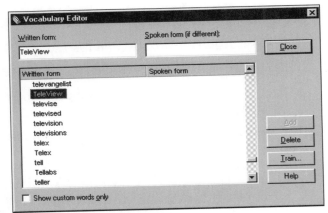

figure A-6

Use the *Vocabulary Editor*
to Delete or Retrain
Incorrect Words

The *Vocabulary Editor* is often used to delete a word that was accidentally misspelled as it was added to a personal speech profile.

Use the *Vocabulary Builder*

Document analysis is one of the most powerful ways to add words to your NaturallySpeaking vocabulary. If you have written a wide variety of reports, particularly those with technical terms or computer jargon, you can analyze the documents in the following way:

1. Create a list of words you wish to train, as shown in Figure A-7, then save your file. It is best to save this file in a simple **.txt** format. (**NOTE:** In Figure A-7, several strategic business units of a fictitious corporation have been listed. These words are unique and are not found in any dictionary.)

figure A-7

Create a List of Words You
Wish to Train

2. Open NaturallySpeaking and say *(Click) NaturallySpeaking → Advanced → Build Vocabulary*.

3. Read the instructions in the **Vocabulary Builder** window (Figure A-8) carefully, because there are many parts to this process. Click the **Next** button when you wish to continue. (**NOTE:** The subsequent screen is optional and you can move to the next step by simply clicking **Next**.) Continue until you see a screen similar to Figure A-9.

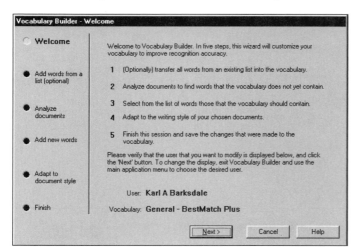

figure A-8

Read the Instructions
Carefully (This Procedure
Can Be Confusing for New
NaturallySpeaking Users)

4. To begin the process of analyzing the words in the file you created in Step 1, click the **Add** button, as shown in Figure A-9. This will allow you to search for and select the document you previously saved. (**NOTE:** You may add any other documents you have created by clicking the **Add** button again and repeating the process.)

5. Highlight any of the documents in the **Document** list that you wish to analyze, as shown in Figure A-9.

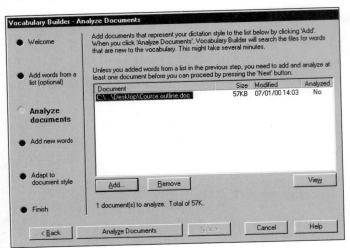

figure A-9

Add Documents You Wish to Analyze

6. Select the **Analyze Documents** button to start your analysis of the words you use.

7. Place a check mark by any word you wish to train and add to your vocabulary (as shown in Figure A-10), then click the **Add Checked Words to Vocabulary** button.. You will then be given a chance to record the words in the normal way. Read the on-screen instructions and save these updates to your speech file. These newly recorded words are now a permanent part of your NaturallySpeaking vocabulary.

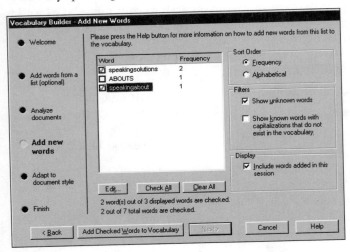

figure A-10

Use the **Add New Words** Window to Select New Words for Recording

F Y I   The remainder of the sections listed on the first page of this appendix can be found online at www.speakingabout.com (click the **Dragon NaturallySpeaking** link):

Ⓓ Making Macros

Ⓔ Manipulating Windows

Dragon NaturallySpeaking Reference Card

Lesson 1 *Up and Running*

1a

Adjust Your Microphone Position

With a headset, place the microphone a thumb's width away from the side of your mouth, or even with or slightly below your lower lip. With a freestanding microphone, you should be within two feet of the receiving device.

- Place your microphone in the same position every time you dictate.

If you notice "breathing errors" (if extra words appear because of your breathing), move your microphone slightly further down below your lower lip or more to the side of your mouth.

1b

Complete Your Enrollment Training

If you are the first user of NaturallySpeaking on your computer, your software will walk you step by step through the enrollment process.   If you are not the first user:

- Start NaturallySpeaking by selecting **Start → Programs → Dragon NaturallySpeaking**.
  - Second User: Choose **Advanced → Manage Users**.
  - Third or Later User: Select **New** from the **Manage Users** dialog box.
- Read and follow the steps that appear on your screen. During training you will:
  - Create your personal speech profile
  - Adjust your microphone
  - Train NaturallySpeaking to understand your way of speaking
  - View the tutorial
  - Start using NaturallySpeaking

1c

Choose Your User Profile

If multiple users are using the same computer:

Choose your name from the **Manage Users** dialog box.

Note It sometimes helps to restart your computer before selecting your user name. This clears any open applications and refreshes system memory allocations.

1d

Readjust Your Audio Settings

Readjust your audio settings if you notice a drop in your recognition accuracy! To run the **Check Audio** utility:

1. Say or choose *(Click) NaturallySpeaking → Advanced → Check Audio*.

2. Read and follow the instructions. You should receive an "Adequate" or higher level on the Quality Check. If you don't, investigate the quality of your headset or the compatibility of your sound card.

Lesson 2 *Practicing Your Enunciation*

2a

✓ Speak Microphone Commands Clearly

Go to Sleep will pause the microphone.

Wake Up will wake the microphone up again.

Microphone Off will turn the microphone completely off. Click the microphone back on again by pressing the **+** key on your numeric keypad.

2b

✓ Speak Words Clearly

- Speak each word clearly.
- Don't break words into syllables. For instance, say **popcorn**, not **pop corn**.
- Don't run words together. Say **candy bar**, not **canybr**.
- Speak continuously. Continue talking until you reach the end of your sentence, thought, or idea.
- Don't speak too fast. Don't speak too slowly. Speak at a speed that is just right for you!
- If extra words randomly appear, move the microphone *slightly* down or to the side and redo your audio check again.
- Don't shout and don't whisper. Don't let your speaking volume trail off toward the end of a sentence.

2c

✓ Clear the Screen

Select All or ***Select Document*** will select all the text in the document.

Delete That will delete the text.

or

Close open documents, then say or click ***(Click) File → New*** to open up a new dictation window.

2d

✓ Speak Line and Paragraph Commands Clearly

New Paragraph is equivalent to pressing the Enter key twice to create a double space.

New Line is like pressing the Enter key once to create a single space.

2e

✓ Speak Punctuation Clearly and Listen to Your Speech

Period creates a (.)

Comma creates a (,)

Question Mark creates a (?)

Dragon NaturallySpeaking for the Office Professional by Karl Barksdale and Michael Rutter. Reference Card ©2001 by Delmar.

Exclamation Point or **Exclamation Mark** creates a (!)

Colon creates a (:)

Semicolon creates a (;)

Dash creates a (-)

Open Quote creates a beginning quote (")

Close Quote creates an ending quote (")

To listen to your document, click or say **Read Document** or select the text and say **Read That**. (**Note:** These two commands only work with the *Preferred* and *Professional* versions of Dragon NaturallySpeaking.)

Commands for moving through a document:

> **Go to Top**
>
> **Go to Bottom**
>
> **Go/Move to Beginning of Line**
>
> **Go/Move to End of Line**

2f

Save Documents

Say *(Click)* **File** <pause> **Save** or **Save As** or choose **File → Save** or **Save As**. Name the file and say or click **Save**.

Lesson 3 *Correcting Speech Errors Immediately*

3a

Scratch or Undo Errors Immediately

Scratch That erases the last continuous phrase you have spoken and can be used multiple times.

Undo That undoes the last mistake or correction you have just dictated; it can reinstate deleted text as well.

3b

Substitute Words

Select <word or words>

(Say the new word or words)

Note Don't pause between the command **Select** and the word or words you are selecting.

Deselect Words and Use *Resume With*

Unselect That will deselect your selection.

Move Right/Left 1 (Character) will unselect any text you have selected.

Resume With **<word or words>** will delete everything following your insertion point. You can start dictating again from that point on.

Select and Delete Errors

Delete That

Select Again

Techniques for getting to the right word in your document:

Select Again

Say ***Select*** **<word>**

Select **<several words>** (or a phrase adjacent to the word you wish to select)

Select the word with your mouse

Spell Web and Email Addresses and the Alphabet

Say ***Press*** and then any letter or key on your keyboard, as in ***Press*** **a** to type the letter **a.**

No Caps On will prevent letters from being capitalized.

No Caps Off will allow letters to be capitalized again.

http will signal to NaturallySpeaking that this is a web address. The *://* punctuation marks will be added automatically and don't need to be stated.

www will also signal to NaturallySpeaking that this is a web address. The *http://* phrase won't be added.

Dot creates a period in web addresses.

Say ***(Press) Backspace*** to delete a letter.

Examples:

   No Caps On **http** **w w w** ***Dot*** **disney** ***Dot*** **com** ***No Caps Off*** = *http://www.disney.com*

   No Caps On **w w w** ***Dot*** **yahoo** ***Dot*** **com** ***No Caps Off*** = *www.yahoo.com*

   No Caps On **miller at speaking about** ***Dot*** **com** ***No Caps Off*** = *miller@speakingabout.com*

To use the military or phonetic alphabet, say ***Press*** followed by . . .

Alpha	Bravo	Charlie	Delta	Echo	Foxtrot	Golf	Hotel	India
Juliet	Kilo	Lima	Mike	November	Oscar	Papa	Quebec	Romeo
Sierra	Tango	Uniform	Victor	Whiskey	X-ray	Yankee	Zulu	

| *Dragon NaturallySpeaking for the Office Professional* by Karl Barksdale and Michael Rutter. Reference Card ©2001 by Delmar.

Lesson 4 *Training Speech Errors Permanently*

4a

Train New Words by Spelling Them

Say *Spell*.

Spell the word letter by letter.

Say *Backspace* to delete a letter.

Say *(Click) Train* or click the **Train** button to train a word.

Say *(Click) Record* and record the word; say *(Click) Done*, *(Click) OK* to finish the process.

4b

Train Words with the *Correction* Window

Say *Select <incorrect word(s)>*.

Say *Spell That* or *Correct That*.

Spell the word(s) letter by letter.

Say *Backspace* to delete a letter.

Use the *Cap* or *Caps On/Off* command for capital letters.

Say *(Click) Train* or choose the **Train** button to open the *Train Words* window.

Say *(Click) Record* or choose the **Record** button to record the word.

Say *(Click) Done*, *(Click) OK* to continue dictating.

4c

Train Names with the *Add Individual Word* Feature

Say *(Click) NaturallySpeaking*, *Words*, *Add Individual Word*.

Spell the name, word, or phrase letter by letter.

Say *Space Bar* to create a space.

Say *Backspace* to delete a letter.

Use the *Cap* command for capital letters.

Say *(Click) Add* or choose the **Add** button to train a word.

Say *(Click) Record* or choose the **Record** button to record a word.

Record the new word, phrase, or name and say *(Click) Done*.

4d

Learn to Use the *Quick Correct* List Alternatives

After the **Quick Correct** list opens, you have two alternatives:

Alternative 1. If the correct alternative appears in the **Quick Correct** list, use the *Choose <number>* command to choose it from the list. Say *Choose 1, 2, 3, 4, or 5* to replace the incorrect word.

Or

Alternative 2. If the correct alternative does not appear in the **Quick Correct** list, or if you feel the word needs to be trained permanently, use the *Spell That* command to open the **Correction** window to spell and record the word.

Transfer Your Correction Dialog Skills to Microsoft Word or Corel WordPerfect

Use the following steps to correct your errors in Microsoft Word or Corel WordPerfect:

A. Speak in complete sentences.

B. Look for mistakes in your completed sentences.

C. Select mistakes using the **Correct <mistake>** command.

D. After the **Correction** window opens, you have two alternatives:

Alternative 1. Use the **Choose <number>** command to choose the correct alternative from the list.

Or

Alternative 2. Spell the word out letter by letter. If the correct word appears while you are spelling, use the **Select <number>** command to avoid having to spell out the entire word.

E. Train the word by saying *(Click) Train That*.

Lesson 5 *Correcting Capitalization*

5a

Capitalize Text

Cap

Cap That or *Capitalize That*

Caps On/Off

5b

Uppercase Text

All Caps

All Caps That

All Caps On/Off

5c

Lowercase Text

No Caps

No Caps That

No Caps On/Off

5d

Capitalize and Compound Words

Compound That

RC-6   *Dragon NaturallySpeaking for the Office Professional* by Karl Barksdale and Michael Rutter. Reference Card ©2001 by Delmar.

Lesson 6 *Creating Symbols and Special Characters*

6a

Say All of the Funny Characters

Symbol or Character	Say
'	**Apostrophe**
's	**Apostrophe S**
`	**Back Quote**
\	**Back Slash**
{	**Open Brace,** or **Left Brace**
}	**Close Brace,** or **Right Brace**
[	**Open Bracket,** or **Left Bracket**
]	**Close Bracket,** or **Right Bracket**
"	**Open Quote,** or **Begin Quotes**
"	**Close Quote,** or **End Quotes**
'	**Open Single Quote,** or **Begin Single Quote**
'	**Close Single Quote,** or **End Single Quote**
:	**Colon**
;	**Semicolon**
,	**Comma**
?	**Question Mark**
!	**Exclamation Point,** or **Exclamation Mark**
–	**Dash** (NOTE: Your dash may appear as two hyphens: --.)
.	**Period,** or **Dot,** or **Point**
...	**Ellipsis**
-	**Hyphen** (NOTE: Select multiple words and say **Hyphenate That** to add hyphens between words after they have been said.)
(	**Open Paren,** or **Open Parenthesis,** or **Left Parenthesis**

Symbol or Character	Say
)	**Close Paren,** or **Close Parenthesis,** or **Right Parenthesis**
/	**Slash,** or **Forward Slash**
	Space Bar, or **Press Space Bar** *(This adds a blank space.)*
~	**Tilde** (NOTE: If you have trouble, try saying **Til-dah** or **Til-day**.)
@	**At Sign**
$	**Dollar Sign**
€	**Euro Sign**
£	**Pound Sterling Sign**
©	**Copyright Sign**
™	**Trademark Sign**
®	**Registered Sign**
°	**Degree Sign**
^	**Caret**
#	**Number Sign,** or **Pound Sign**
*	**Asterisk**
%	**Percent Sign**
<	**Open Angle Bracket,** or **Less Than**
>	**Close Angle Bracket,** or **Greater Than**
&	**Ampersand**
_	**Underscore**
|	**Vertical Bar**
+	**Plus Sign**
-	**Minus Sign**
=	**Equals Sign,** or **Equals**

Dragon NaturallySpeaking for the Office Professional by Karl Barksdale and Michael Rutter. Reference Card ©2001 by Delmar.

Lesson 7 *Generating Numbers*

7a

Say Single Digits

Say the numbers 0-9 normally.

If you have difficulty, say **Numeral <number>**.

If you have difficulty dictating numbers, you can use the numbers mode. You can say either **Start Numbers Mode** or **Numbers Mode On** before you say the numbers, then say **Stop Numbers Mode** or **Numbers Mode Off** to go back to normal mode.

7b

Say Double Digits and Beyond

Say numbers 10 and higher normally.   For example:

ten = *10*   **fifteen =** *15*   **twenty-two** = *22*   **ninety-seven** = *97*   **two hundred fifty-five** = *255*

two million five hundred twenty-eight thousand two hundred eighty-one = *2,528,281*

7c

Say Decimals and Fractions

Say the number, **Point**, and another number, as in: **two** **Point** **seven** = *2.7*   **six** **Point** **five seven** = *6.57*

Say fractions normally, as in **one half** or **five sixteenths**.

Or

Say the first number (numerator), **Slash**, and the second number (denominator): **1** **Slash** **4** = *1/4*

7d

Say Dates

Say the month, the date, a comma, and the year. For example:

July fourth **Comma** **seventeen seventy-six** = *July 4, 1776*

January first **Comma** **two thousand five** = *January 1, 2005*

To say dates in the numeric format, say: **twelve** **Slash** **seven** **Slash** **oh seven** = *12/7/07*

7e

Say Phone Numbers

Say the numbers naturally, pausing slightly where the hyphens go, but don't say the hyphens.   You *will* need to say the parentheses. For example, say:

one **Open Paren** **seven six five** **Close Paren** **five five five oh one eight two** = *1 (765) 555-0182*

 Dragon NaturallySpeaking for the Office Professional by Karl Barksdale and Michael Rutter. Reference Card ©2001 by Delmar.

Say Currency

Say currency normally, as in:

Four dollars = *$4.00*   **Five dollars and seventy-five cents** = *$5.75*

One million two hundred thirty-seven dollars and ninety-five cents = *$1,000,237.95*

Say Times of Day

Here's how to say a time that includes either **AM** or **PM**:

Ten thirty AM = *10:30 AM*   **Ten thirty PM** = *10:30 PM*

If you say **o'clock**, your times will appear as follows:

Ten o'clock = *10:00*   **Two o'clock** = *2:00*

Say Math Formulas

Say *Plus Sign* for +

Say *Minus Sign* for –

Say *Asterisk* for * (for times)

Say *Slash* for / (for divided by)

Say *Equals Sign* or *Equals* for =

Say **Open Angle Bracket** or **Less Than** for <

Say **Close Angle Bracket** or **Greater Than** for >

To create the following formula, say **two *Plus Sign* two *Equals Sign* four**, or ***Numeral* two *Plus Sign* *Numeral* two *Equals Sign* *Numeral* four**:

$2 + 2 = 4$

Say Roman Numerals

Say *Roman* **<number>** to create a Roman numeral.

Create Numbered Lists

Numeral **1** *Period Space Bar Space Bar* (Now say the first listed item.)

Numeral **2** *Period Space Bar Space Bar* (Now say the second listed item.)

Format Numbers as Text or Numerals

If text appears instead of a numeral, select it and say *Format That Number*.

If a numeral appears instead of text, select it and say *Format That Spelled Out*.

Lesson 8 *Navigating Documents*

8b

Move Character by Character

Move Right /Forward 1-20 Character(s)

Move Left /Back 1-20 Character(s)

When moving one character at a time, you can say **Move Right/Left a Character**, or **Move Right/Left 1 Character.** The word **Characters** is often optional when you use the **Right** and **Left** commands in some programs like Microsoft Word.

8c

Move Word by Word

Move Right/Forward 1-20 Word(s)

Move Left/Back 1-20 Word(s)

When moving one word at a time, you can say either **Move Right/Left a Word** or **Move Right/Left 1 Word.**

8d

Move Line by Line

Move Up 1-20 (Line(s))

Move Down 1-20 (Line(s))

Move Back 1-20 Line(s)

Move Forward 1-20 Line(s)

The word **Lines** is optional with the **Up** and **Down** commands. Say **Lines** if the system seems to hang up. When moving up or down one line at a time, you can say either **Move Up/Down a Line** or **Move Up/Down 1 Line**.

8e

Move Paragraph by Paragraph and to Beginning and End

Go to Top

Go to Bottom

Move to/Go to Beginning/Start of Line

Move to/Go to End of Line

Move to/Go to Beginning/Start of Document

Move to/Go to Bottom of Document

Move Up 1-20 Paragraph(s)

Move Down 1-20 Paragraph(s)

Move Back 1-20 Paragraph(s)

Move Forward 1-20 Paragraph(s)

When moving up or down one paragraph at a time, you can say either **Move Up/Down a Paragraph** or **Move Up/Down 1 Paragraph**. Other options also work, such as **Go/Move to Start/End of Document**.

Lesson 9 *Selecting, Deleting, and Moving Text*

9a

Select and Delete Character by Character

Select Next/Previous Character

Select Next/Forward 1-20 Character(s)

Select Previous/Back/Last 1-20 Character(s)

Delete Next/Previous Character

Delete Next/Forward 1-20 Character(s)

Delete Previous/Back/Last 1-20 Character(s)

Dragon NaturallySpeaking for the Office Professional by Karl Barksdale and Michael Rutter. Reference Card ©2001 by Delmar.

Select and Delete Word by Word

Select <word> Through <word> or *Select <word> to <word>*

Select Next/Previous Word

Select Next/Forward 1-20 Word(s)

Select Previous/Back/Last 1-20 Word(s)

Delete Next/Previous Word

Delete Next/Forward 1-20 Word(s)

Delete Previous/Back/Last 1-20 Word(s)

Select and Delete Line by Line, Paragraph by Paragraph, and from Beginning and End

Select Line

Select Next/Previous Line

Select Next/Forward 1-20 Line(s)

Select Previous/Back/Last 1-20 Line(s)

—

Delete Line

Delete Next/Previous Line

Delete Next/Forward 1-20 Line(s)

Delete Previous/Back/Last 1-20 Line(s)

Select Paragraph

Select Next/Previous Paragraph

Select Next/Forward 1-20 Paragraph(s)

Select Previous/Back/Last 1-20 Paragraph(s)

—

Delete Paragraph

Delete Next/Forward Paragraph

Delete Next/Forward 1-20 Paragraph(s)

Delete Previous/Back/Last 1-20 Paragraph(s)

Copy, Cut, and Paste Blocks of Text

Copy That or *Copy Selection*

Cut That or *Cut Selection*

Paste That

Lesson 10 *Formatting Documents*

Bold Text

Bold That

Restore That or *Format That (Plain/Normal/Regular)*

Italicize Text

Italicize That

Restore That or *Format That (Plain/Normal/Regular)*

Underline Text

Underline That

Restore That or ***Format That (Plain/Normal/Regular)***

Add Bulleted Lists

DragonPad: ***(Click) Format*** <pause> ***Bullet Style***.

Microsoft Word: Click the **Bullets** button or say ***(Click) Format*** <pause> ***Bullets and Numbering***. Choose the **Bulleted** tab with your voice and choose a bullet style by saying ***Move Right/Left*** <number> or ***Move Up/Down*** <number>, then say ***(Click) OK***.

To remove bullets, repeat the steps above.

Align Text and Change Fonts

To align text:

   Center That or ***Format That Centered***

   Left Align That or ***Format That Left Aligned***

   Right Align That or ***Format That Right Aligned***

To change fonts and sizes:

   Set Font <name of font>

   Set Size <number of point size>

   Or

   Set Font <name of font and number of point size>

   Or

   Format That Font <name of font>

Use *What Can I Say?*

What Can I Say? (This command opens the ***What Can I Say?*** help window.)

Transfer Text to Microsoft Word or Other Programs

.rtf   **R**ich **T**ext **F**ormat

.txt   **T**e**XT** Format

.doc   Word **DOC**ument Format

.wpd   **W**ord**P**erfect **D**ocument Format

Copy All to Clipboard will select and copy an entire document. Then ***Paste That*** will transfer the text to your target word processing application.

 Dragon NaturallySpeaking for the Office Professional by Karl Barksdale and Michael Rutter. Reference Card ©2001 by Delmar.